Fast and Easy
C++ Lessons

In This Edition:
Alternative Tokens
and Comments
On Microsoft
Visual Studio Code
in Linux Ubuntu

Zlatin Georgiev

Version 1.1, 2024-04-22

Table Of Contents

Copyright

No part of this book may be reproduced or transmitted, downloaded, distributed, redesigned or stored, or incorporated into any system for the storage and retrieval of information, in any form or by any means, including photocopying and recording, whether electronic or mechanical, now known or invented in the future without the written permission of the author.

Dedication

This book is for those who like to learn new and interesting things.

Introduction

This book will teach you practically:

- How to install tools to build 32-bit and 64-bit **C** and **C++** applications, which is important to reproduce all the examples in the book correctly;
- What are **C** and **C++** primary and alternative operators;
- How you can comment your **C++** source code;
- A brief understanding of commands from the bash scripting language used to automate operations by the operating system;

and many more.

In addition, in separate chapters, the book contains detailed explanations of the sample **C++** program code and the batch scripts used.

All examples in this book were tested on a computer with the **Ubuntu version 22.04.3** operating system at the time immediately before publication.

 The installation of the necessary

tools for compiling and editing **C** and **C++** programs have been carefully tested ($\checkmark$), in case there is a problem with the installation, please double-check the installation script texts and confirm you have typed them in correctly. Make sure you have carefully followed the instructions in the book.

The examples are tested ($\checkmark$) for fluent compilation. In case they do not compile or run, it would be good to ensure the input you entered matches that in the book.

The output results correspond to the examples used (there may be differences in rare cases when some non-standard symbols or graphic characters are output).

The following bookmarks are used in the book:

- to note
- a piece of advice
- bring to attention

⚠️ warning

❗ of importance

Chapter 1. Installing tools for compiling and editing C++ programs

1.1. Installing Linux C++ building tools

To install the necessary tools, press the key combination `Ctrl` + `Alt` + `T`, through which we open the **Linux Terminal**, in which we enter:

> If the **Linux Terminal** does not open:
> **1**. Press the key combination `Ctrl` + `Alt` + `F3`.
> **2**. Log in as `root` with your `root` `password`.
> **3**. Enter the `nano` `/etc/default/locale` and inside the text editor change everywhere the `en_US` to the `en_US.UTF-8` and press `Ctrl` + `S` to save your changes.
> **4**. After that press `Ctrl` + `X` to exit the text editor.
> **5**. Execute the `locale-gen --purge` command and `reboot` to restart the **Linux Ubuntu** operating system.

Listing 1. Linux Terminal

```
echo ${USER}
```

The result of this command is the current `<user name>`. We will use this user name to add the user to the sudoers group with administrator privileges.

Listing 2. Linux Terminal

```
su -
usermod -aG sudo "<the user name from the above echo command>"
reboot
```

After rebooting in a **Linux Terminal**, we enter the command:

Listing 3. Linux Terminal

```
sudo apt -y update
```

After the execution of the above command, we enter the password with which we log in as a user in **Ubuntu** in response to the message [sudo] password for the developer: and press the Enter key.

Listing 4. Linux Terminal

```
sudo apt -y install build-essential
```

The above command installs:

- g++ the GNU compiler for **C++** programs;
- gcc the GNU compiler for **C** programs;
- make utility that is used for directing the building of programs;

and possibly the gdb debugger for Linux

programs.

Listing 5. Linux Terminal

```
sudo apt -y install gdb
```

The above command installs the gdb GNU
debugger.

See the appendixes to find out how you can
install a newer version of **GCC** than the one
installed by default for your particular version
of **Linux**:

- Appendix A, *Installing a newer release version
  of the GNU Compiler Collection (GCC)*

- Appendix B, *Installing the latest version of the
  GNU Compiler Collection (GCC)*

1.1.1. Checking the C++ compiler is properly working

We check if the compiler, for **C++** programs, is properly installed:

We check the **C++** compiler version:

Listing 6. Linux Terminal

```
g++ --version
```

The result we get should look something like this:

Example 1. Default g++ version for **Linux Ubuntu** 22.04 LTS

```
g++ (Ubuntu 11.3.0-1ubuntu1~22.04) 11.3.0
Copyright (C) 2021 Free Software Foundation, Inc.
This is free software; see the source for copying conditions.  There is NO
warranty; not even for MERCHANTABILITY or FITNESS FOR A PARTICULAR PURPOSE.
```

 For the **Linux Ubuntu** 18.x the result looks like the next one:

Example 2. Default g++ version for **Linux Ubuntu** 18.04 LTS

```
g++ (Ubuntu 7.5.0-3ubuntu1~18.04) 7.5.0
Copyright (C) 2017 Free Software Foundation, Inc.
This is free software; see the source for copying conditions.  There is NO
warranty; not even for MERCHANTABILITY or FITNESS FOR A PARTICULAR PURPOSE.
```

Then in the command window, we write:

Listing 7. Linux Terminal

```
which g++
```

to check if the compiler, for **C++** programs, is installed.

Example 3. The result should look something like this:

```
/usr/bin/g++
```

1.1.2. Creating and compiling a C++ Hello World application

The next thing we'll do is create a folder in which to place the `hello_world` application source code with the command:

Listing 8. Linux Terminal

```
mkdir -p ~/c++/sources/chapter_01_01_02/step_01
```

Then we enter the newly created folder:

Listing 9. Linux Terminal

```
cd ~/c++/sources/chapter_01_01_02/step_01
```

In this folder, we create the `hello_world.cpp` file:

Listing 10. Linux Terminal

```
nano hello_world.cpp
```

Listing 11.
~/c++/sources/chapter_01/step_01_01_02/hello_world.cpp

```cpp
#include <iostream>

using namespace std;

int main() {
  cout << "Hello World!\n";
}
```

We enter the program code and save it with the key combination `Ctrl` + `S`, then exit the text editor with `Ctrl` + `X`.

We compile the test program with the command:

Listing 12. Linux Terminal

```
g++ -o hello_world hello_world.cpp
```

then we launch it

Listing 13. Linux Terminal

```
./hello_world
```

Example 4. The result displayed on the screen should be:

```
Hello World!
```

In this way, we verified that we have an environment in which we can create programs written in the programming language **C++**.

After successfully installing the necessary tools to write and compile **C** and **C++** programs for the **Linux** operating system we can proceed to install **Microsoft Visual Studio Code** - a tool for editing and debugging **C++** source code.

Now I will briefly explain what each line of the above program means:

```
#include <iostream>
```

This line loads the **C++** function descriptions to work with input/output streams - in this case, the function `cout`

```
using namespace std;
```

This line specifies that we can use functions from the `std` namespace without specifying their full name, in this case, we can use `cout` instead of `std::cout`, which makes the program code more readable.

 Defaulting to the `std` namespace is bad practice, as this is the **Standard Template Library** namespace of **C++**. The above way of setting default namespaces can be used for namespaces belonging to the particular application being developed.

```
int main() {
```

This line indicates the beginning of the entry point function in the **C++** program. This is the function named `main` which returns an integer `int`. It does not accept input parameters in its current declaration.

> The `main` function can also be declared with two input parameters, one of which specifies the number of arguments passed from the command line of the program, and the other the parameters themselves in the form of an array of strings - for example, `int main(int arguments_count, char* arguments [])` or `int main(int arguments_count, char** arguments)`.

```
cout << "Hello World!\n";
```

This line from the body of the `main` function outputs the `Hello World!` message that we see in the command window after the program is executed.

```
}
```

This line ends the body of the `main` function.

1.2. Installing the Microsoft Visual Studio Code

We will install **Microsoft Visual Studio Code** using the **snap** tool.

1.2.1. Installing the Microsoft Visual Studio Code using the Snap tool

1. We open a new **Linux Terminal** with the key combination `Ctrl + Alt + T`:

2. Before we start the actual installation of **Microsoft Visual Studio Code** we will prepare two settings files that we will need to compile **C++** programs.

    a. We create the folder `~/c++/.vscode`:

    Listing 14. Linux Terminal

    ```
    mkdir -p ~/c++/.vscode
    ```

    b. and the file `~/c++/.vscode/tasks.json`

    Listing 15. Linux Terminal

    ```
    nano ~/c++/.vscode/tasks.json
    ```

     When using `64`-bit operating system **Linux Ubuntu** version `18.04.6` in the script below you should replace `c++20` with `c++17` everywhere. Because in this case the default `build-essential` installs the `g++` version `7.5.0` and it supports the `c++17` standard and below.

with the following content:

Listing 16. `~/c++/.vscode/tasks.json`

```json
{
  "tasks": [
    {
      "type": "cppbuild",
      "label": "C/C++: g++ build active file",
      "command": "/usr/bin/g++",
      "args": [
        "-std=c++20",
        "-Wfatal-errors",
        "-fdiagnostics-color=always",
        "-lstdc++",
        "-I.",
        "-g",
        "${file}",
        "-o",
        "${fileDirname}/${fileBasenameNoExtension}"
      ],
      "options": {
        "cwd": "${fileDirname}"
      },
      "problemMatcher": [
        "$gcc"
      ],
      "group": {
        "kind": "build",
        "isDefault": true
      },
      "detail": "Task generated by Debugger."
    }
  ],
  "version": "2.0.0"
}
```

and save it with `Ctrl` + `S` and you can close the nano text editor with `Ctrl` + `X`.

c. We also create the file `~/c++/.vscode/launch.json` in the same folder:

Listing 17. Linux Terminal

```
nano ~/c++/.vscode/launch.json
```

and in it, we enter the following content:

Listing 18. `~/c++/.vscode/launch.json`

```json
{
  "version": "0.2.0",
  "configurations": [
   {
     "name": "(gdb) Launch",
     "type": "cppdbg",
     "request": "launch",
     "program": "${fileDirname}/${fileBasenameNoExtension}",
     "args": [],
     "stopAtEntry": false,
     "cwd": "${workspaceFolder}",
     "externalConsole": false,
     "MIMode": "gdb",
     "setupCommands": [
       {
         "description": "Enable pretty-printing for gdb",
         "text": "-enable-pretty-printing",
         "ignoreFailures": true
       },
       {
         "description": "Set Disassembly Flavor to Intel",
         "text": "-gdb-set disassembly-flavor intel",
         "ignoreFailures": true
       }
     ],
     "additionalSOLibSearchPath": "",
     "preLaunchTask": "C/C++: g++ build active file"
   }
  ]
}
```

and save it with `Ctrl` + `S`. After that close the `nano` text editor with `Ctrl` + `X`.

d. Then we create a configuration file for automatic formatting of C++ source code `~/c++/.clang-format`

Listing 19. Linux Terminal

```
nano ~/c++/.clang-format
```

with content:

Listing 20. `~/c++/.clang-format`

```
---
Language:                       Cpp
Standard:                       Cpp03
BasedOnStyle:                   Chromium
ColumnLimit:                    120
UseTab:                         Never
AlignConsecutiveAssignments:    true
---
Language:                       Json
BasedOnStyle:                   Chromium
IndentWidth:                    1
...
```

and save it using the key combination `Ctrl` + `S` and close the nano text editor with `Ctrl` + `X`.

3. Next, we install **Microsoft Visual Studio Code** using **snap**

Listing 21. Linux Terminal

```
sudo apt -y install snapd
sudo snap install --classic code
```

4. When the installation is finished we install the extension to **Microsoft Visual Studio**

Code, which allows us to compile and debug C++ programs.

Listing 22. Linux Terminal

```
code --install-extension ms-vscode.cpptools-extension-pack
```

> ℹ Installing the extensions this way, from the command line, allows you to automate the process with the help of scripts for the operating system, so you will easily have all the extensions that are convenient and necessary for you to work, even if you have to reinstall **Microsoft Visual Studio Code**.

5. Then we run **Microsoft Visual Studio Code** so that it opens the folder ~/c++ and the file hello_world.cpp:

Listing 23. Linux Terminal

```
code ~/c++ ~/c++/sources/chapter_01_01_02/step_01/hello_world.cpp
```

> ℹ This is a very convenient feature of **Microsoft Visual Studio Code** that allows you to launch it with the working folder and file you need to edit, directly from the command line, without having to

specify them later in the working environment itself with a mouse or keyboard commands. For example, you can make a script that automates the opening of a working folder and file for each of the applications you develop.

6. At the first launch, we will answer the question `Do you trust the authors of the files in the folder?` by pressing the `[Yes, I trust the authors]` button:

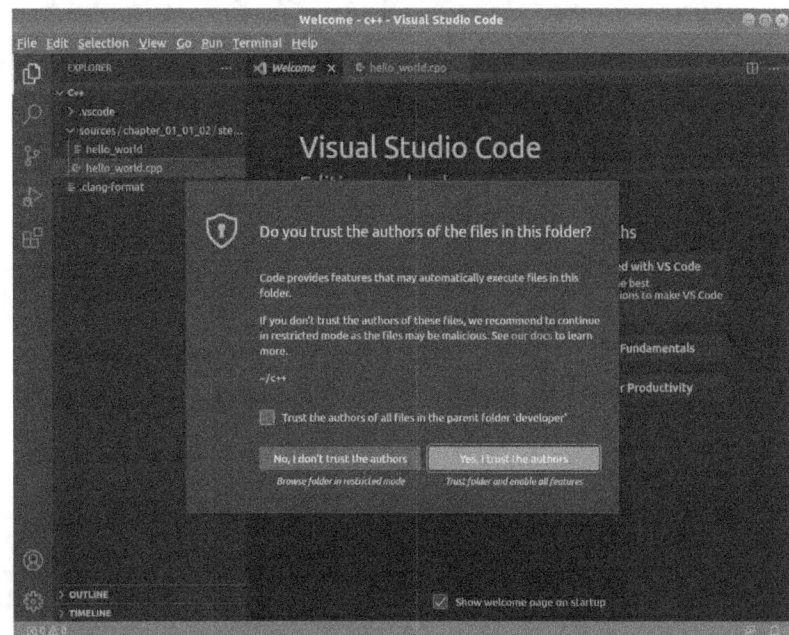

Figure 1. Do you trust the authors of the files in the folder?

7. After that, the `Welcome` screen of the program appears and we close it with `Ctrl` + `W`:

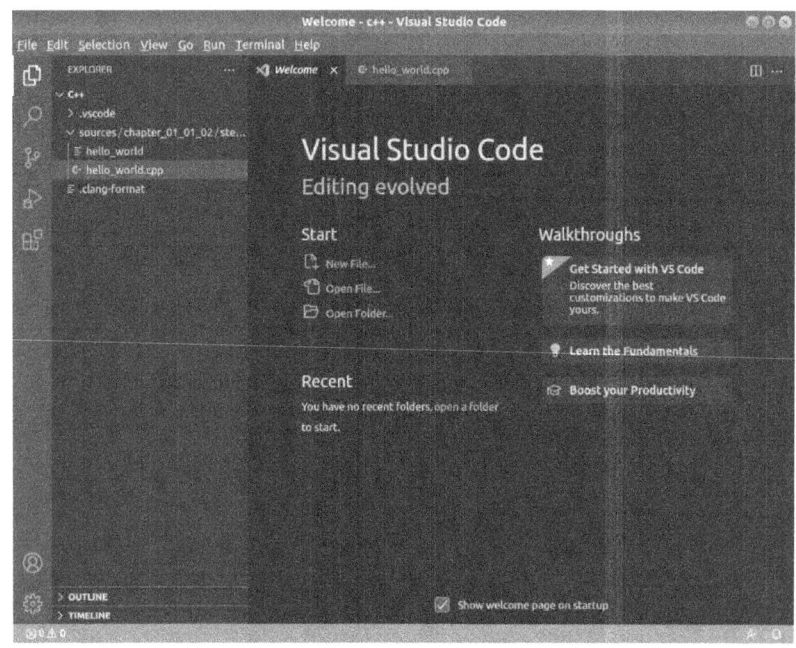

Figure 2. **Microsoft Visual Studio Code** *Welcome screen*

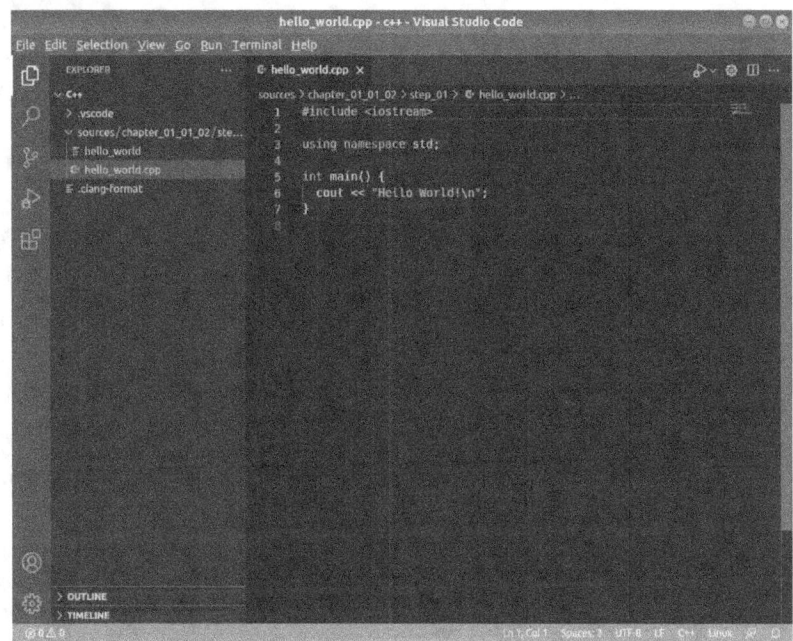

Figure 3. **Microsoft Visual Studio Code** *opening*
`hello_world.cpp`

8. Then we press the `F5` key, which will allow us to compile the program and run it in trace mode. We will see execution in the DEBUG CONSOLE:

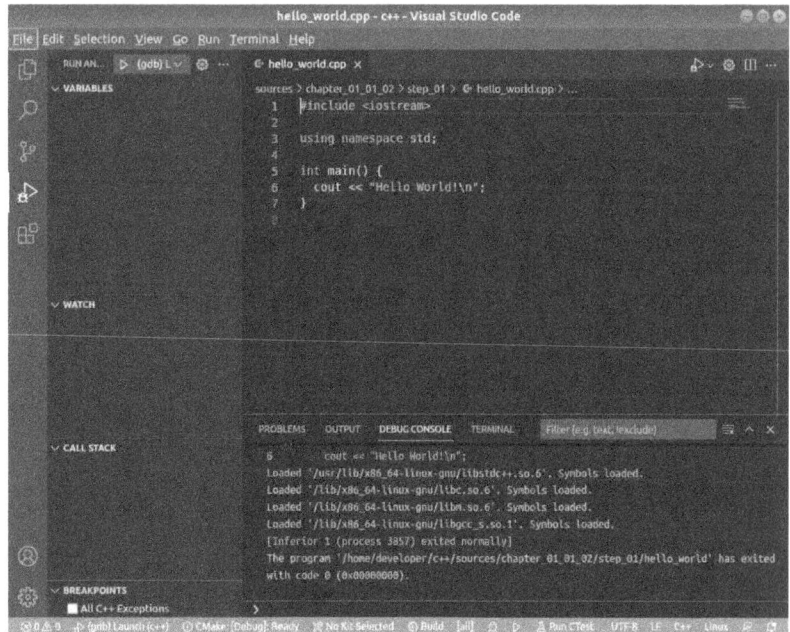

Figure 4. Run with the F5 key in the debug console

9. We will see the result of the execution of the `Hello World!` program in the Microsoft Visual Studio Code `TERMINAL` window by clicking the [`left mouse button`] on it.

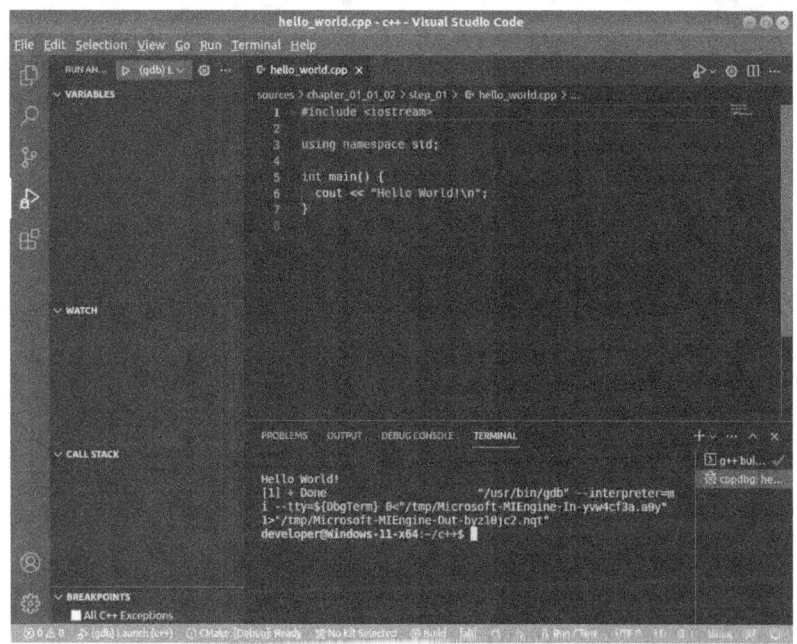

Figure 5. **Microsoft Visual Studio Code** *terminal window*

If we want to trace the execution of a program, we simply click the [left mouse button] in front of the number of the line at which we want the execution to stop and there appears a red dot - a breakpoint. Then we press the F5 key again and the program compiles to an executable again and stops its execution at the line with the red dot. To continue execution:

- We can press F5 again to continue to the next breakpoint or until the end of the program.

- We can also use the F10 key to execute the code of the current line and stop the execution of the next line.

- It is also possible to use the `F11` key to examine the execution of the current function.

If we want to remove a breakpoint, we simply click the [`left mouse button`] on the `red dot` and it disappears.

Having successfully installed the necessary tools for compiling and tracing **C++** programs will allow us to compile all the examples in this book.

Chapter 2. Alternative Tokens

Alternatives are provided for some operators and characters in the **C++** language. From the point of view of the **C++** compiler, the main and alternate characters and operators are equivalent. In the table below, I have presented the main and alternative operators and characters along with a brief description of their purpose in the **C++** programming language.

Primary	Alternative	Description
[	<:	opening square bracket
]	:>	closing square bracket
{	<%	opening figure bracket
}	%>	closing figure bracket
#	%:	sharp
##	%:%:	double sharp
&&	and	logically and
&	bitand	bitwise and
&=	and_eq	bitwise and with acquisition
||	or	logical or

Primary	Alternative	Description
|	bitor	bitwise or
|=	or_eq	bitwise or with acquisition
^	xor	bitwise exclusionary or
^=	xor_eq	bitwise exclusionary or with acquisition
!	not	logical negation
!=	not_eq	logical negation with acquisition
~	compl	bitwise compliment

In the following sections, I will show with examples the action and meaning of each character and operator from the above table.

2.1. Opening and Closing Square Brackets

The opening and closing square brackets are used to enclose indexes or keys of arrays, sets, maps, or other specialized structures.

I'll show you how you can replace the basic and alternate variations of the square brackets.

We create a folder in which to put the source code of the program.

Listing 24. Linux Terminal

```
mkdir -p ~/c++/sources/chapter_02_01_00/square_brackets_01
```

Then we enter the newly created folder.

Listing 25. Linux Terminal

```
cd ~/c++/sources/chapter_02_01_00/square_brackets_01
```

In this folder, we create the file `main.cpp`

Listing 26. Linux Terminal

```
code main.cpp
```

With the following content:

Listing 27. `chapter_02_01_00/square_brackets_01/main.cpp`

```
#include <array>
```

```cpp
#include <iostream>

int main() {
  std::array<int, 3> int_array{1, 2, 3};

  std::cout << "Primary square brackets '[ ... ]'\n";
  for (int index = 0, size = int_array.size(); index < size; ++index) {
    std::cout << "int_array[ " << index << " ] = ";
    std::cout << int_array[index] << "\n";
  }
  std::cout << "\n";

  std::cout << "Alternative square brackets '<: ... :>'\n";
  for (int index = 0, size = int_array.size(); index < size; ++index) {
    std::cout << "int_array<: " << index << " :> = ";
    std::cout << int_array <: index :> << "\n";
  }
  std::cout << "\n";

  std::cout << "Open primary, close alternative square brackets '[ ... :>'\n";
  for (int index = 0, size = int_array.size(); index < size; ++index) {
    std::cout << "int_array[ " << index << " :> = ";
    std::cout << int_array[index:> << "\n";
  }
  std::cout << "\n";

  std::cout << "Open alternative, close primary square brackets '<: ... ]'\n";
  for (int index = 0, size = int_array.size(); index < size; ++index) {
    std::cout << "int_array<: " << index << " ] = ";
    std::cout << int_array<:index] << "\n";
  }
  std::cout << std::endl;

  return EXIT_SUCCESS;
}
```

We compile the test program by running the command:

Listing 28. Linux Terminal

```
g++ -o main main.cpp
```

then we launch it

Listing 29. Linux Terminal

```
./main
```

Example 5. The result of the execution that is displayed on the screen should be the following:

```
Primary square brackets '[ ... ]'
int_array[ 0 ] = 1
int_array[ 1 ] = 2
int_array[ 2 ] = 3

Alternative square brackets '<: ... :>'
int_array<: 0 :> = 1
int_array<: 1 :> = 2
int_array<: 2 :> = 3

Open primary, close alternative square brackets '[ ... :>'
int_array[ 0 :> = 1
int_array[ 1 :> = 2
int_array[ 2 :> = 3

Open alternative, close primary square brackets '<: ... ]'
int_array<: 0 ] = 1
int_array<: 1 ] = 2
int_array<: 2 ] = 3
```

We execute the command,

Listing 30. Linux Terminal

```
echo $?
```

which outputs the result returned by the executable.

Example 6. The value should be:

```
0
```

2.2. Opening and Closing Figure Brackets

Curly braces enclose a namespace, a program block, a class or structure declaration, and variable or constant initialization.

I'll show you how you can replace the basic and alternate variations of the figure brackets.

We create a folder in which to put the source code of the program.

Listing 31. Linux Terminal

```
mkdir -p ~/c++/sources/chapter_02_02_00/figure_brackets_01
```

Then we enter the newly created folder.

Listing 32. Linux Terminal

```
cd ~/c++/sources/chapter_02_02_00/figure_brackets_01
```

In this folder, we create the file main.cpp

Listing 33. Linux Terminal

```
code main.cpp
```

With the following content:

Listing 34. chapter_02_02_00/figure_brackets_01/main.cpp

```
#include <cstdlib>   // EXIT_SUCCESS
```

```cpp
#include <cstring>   // strchr
#include <iostream>  // std::cout, <<, std::endl
#include <typeinfo>  // typeid

//
// primary namespace braces
//
namespace curly_braces {

// function definitions
void primary_function_definition() {
  std::cout << __FUNCTION__ << "( ... ) { ... }\n";
}
void alternative_function_definition() <%
  std::cout << __FUNCTION__ << "( ... ) <% ... %>\n";
%>

}  // namespace curly_braces
using namespace curly_braces;

//
// alternative namespace braces
//
namespace helpers <%

std::string remove_leading_numbers(std::string const& value) {
  size_t index = 0;

  if (value.length() > 0) {
    while (strchr("0123456789", value.at(index)) != nullptr) {
      ++index;
    }
  }

  std::string result = value.substr(index);

  return result;
}  // namespace std::stringremove_leading_numbers(std::stringconst&value)

%>  // namespace helpers
using namespace helpers;

// class definitions:
class Primary_Figure_Brackets_Class_Definition {
 public:
  Primary_Figure_Brackets_Class_Definition() {
    std::cout << remove_leading_numbers(typeid(*this).name()) << " { ... };\n";
  }
};
class Alternative_Figure_Brackets_Class_Definition <%
 public:
  Alternative_Figure_Brackets_Class_Definition() {
```

```cpp
      std::cout << remove_leading_numbers(typeid(*this).name()) << " <% ... %>;\n";
  }
%>;

// structure definitions:
struct Primary_Figure_Brackets_Structure_Definition {
  Primary_Figure_Brackets_Structure_Definition() {
    std::cout << remove_leading_numbers(typeid(*this).name()) << " { ... };\n";
  }
};
struct Alternative_Figure_Brackets_Structure_Definition <%
  Alternative_Figure_Brackets_Structure_Definition() {
    std::cout << remove_leading_numbers(typeid(*this).name()) << " <% ... %>;\n";
  }
%>;

int main() {
  primary_function_definition();
  alternative_function_definition();
  std::cout << "\n";

  const Primary_Figure_Brackets_Class_Definition
      primary_figure_brackets_class_definition;
  const Alternative_Figure_Brackets_Class_Definition
      alternative_figure_brackets_class_definition;
  Primary_Figure_Brackets_Structure_Definition
      primary_figure_brackets_structure_definition;
  Alternative_Figure_Brackets_Structure_Definition
      alternative_figure_brackets_structure_definition;
  std::cout << "\n";

  int number = 10;

  std::cout << "Primary figure brackets '{ " << number << " }'\n";

  <%
    int number = 20;

    std::cout << "Alternative figure brackets ";
    std::cout << "'<% ";
    std::cout << number;
    std::cout << " %>'\n";
  %>

  {
    int number = 30;

    std::cout << "Primary open, alternative close figure brackets ";
    std::cout << "'{ ";
    std::cout << number;
    std::cout << " %>'\n";
  %>
```

```
<%
  int number = 40;

  std::cout << "Alternative open, primary close figure brackets ";
  std::cout << "'<% ";
  std::cout << number;
  std::cout << " }'\n";
}

std::cout << "Primary figure brackets '{ " << number << " }'\n\n";

// constant initialization:
const int primary_initialized_integer_constant{1};
std::cout << "primary_initialized_integer_constant{ "
          << primary_initialized_integer_constant << " }\n";
const int alternative_initialized_integer_constant<% 2 %>;
std::cout << "alternative_initialized_integer_constant<% "
          << alternative_initialized_integer_constant << " %>\n\n";

// variable initialization:
int primary_initialized_integer_variable{3};
std::cout << "primary_initialized_integer_variable{ "
          << primary_initialized_integer_variable << " }\n";
int alternative_initialized_integer_variable<% 4 %>;
std::cout << "alternative_initialized_integer_variable<% "
          << alternative_initialized_integer_variable << " %>" << std::endl;

  return EXIT_SUCCESS;
}
```

We compile the test program by running the command:

Listing 35. Linux Terminal

```
g++ -o main main.cpp
```

then we launch it

Listing 36. Linux Terminal

```
./main
```

Example 7. The result of the execution that is displayed on the screen should be the following:

```
primary_function_definition( ... ) { ... }
alternative_function_definition( ... ) <% ... %>

Primary_Figure_Brackets_Class_Definition { ... };
Alternative_Figure_Brackets_Class_Definition <% ... %>;
Primary_Figure_Brackets_Structure_Definition { ... };
Alternative_Figure_Brackets_Structure_Definition <% ... %>;

Primary figure brackets '{ 10 }'
Alternative figure brackets '<% 20 %>'
Primary open, alternative close figure brackets '{ 30 %>'
Alternative open, primary close figure brackets '<% 40 }'
Primary figure brackets '{ 10 }'

primary_initialized_integer_constant{ 1 }
alternative_initialized_integer_constant<% 2 %>

primary_initialized_integer_variable{ 3 }
alternative_initialized_integer_variable<% 4 %>
```

We execute the command,

Listing 37. Linux Terminal

```
echo $?
```

which outputs the result returned by the executable.

Example 8. The value should be:

```
0
```

2.3. Sharp

Sharp is normally used in preprocessing commands.

I'll show you how you can replace the basic and alternate variations of the sharp sign.

We create a folder in which to put the source code of the program.

Listing 38. Linux Terminal

```
mkdir -p ~/c++/sources/chapter_02_03_00/sharp_01
```

Then we enter the newly created folder.

Listing 39. Linux Terminal

```
cd ~/c++/sources/chapter_02_03_00/sharp_01
```

In this folder, we create the file main.cpp

Listing 40. Linux Terminal

```
code main.cpp
```

With the following content:

Listing 41. chapter_02_03_00/sharp_01/main.cpp

```
#include <iostream>

// primary sharp
#define TEXT_PRIMARY(item) #item

// alternative sharp
```

```
%:define TEXT_ALTERNATIVE(item) %:item

int main() {
  int integer_value = 10;

  std::cout << "'#'  " << TEXT_PRIMARY(integer_value) << " = " << integer_value
            << "\n";
  std::cout << "'%:' " << TEXT_ALTERNATIVE(integer_value) << " = "
            << integer_value << "\n\n";

#ifdef _WIN32
  std::cout << "Hello from Windows!" << std::endl;
%:else
  std::cout << "Hello from alternative sharp!" << std::endl;
%:endif

  return EXIT_SUCCESS;
}
```

We compile the test program by running the command:

Listing 42. Linux Terminal

```
g++ -o main main.cpp
```

then we launch it

Listing 43. Linux Terminal

```
./main
```

Example 9. The result of the execution that is displayed on the screen should be the following:

```
'#'  integer_value = 10
'%:' integer_value = 10

Hello from alternative sharp!
```

We execute the command,

Listing 44. Linux Terminal

```
echo $?
```

which outputs the result returned by the executable.

Example 10. The value should be:

```
0
```

2.4. Double Sharp

Double sharp is normally used for concatenating in preprocessing commands.

I'll show you how you can replace the basic and alternate variations of the double sharp sign.

We create a folder in which to put the source code of the program.

Listing 45. Linux Terminal

```
mkdir -p ~/c++/sources/chapter_02_04_00/double_sharp_01
```

Then we enter the newly created folder.

Listing 46. Linux Terminal

```
cd ~/c++/sources/chapter_02_04_00/double_sharp_01
```

In this folder, we create the file main.cpp

Listing 47. Linux Terminal

```
code main.cpp
```

With the following content:

Listing 48. chapter_02_04_00/double_sharp_01/main.cpp

```cpp
#include <iostream>

#define STICK_PRIMARY(item_left_part, item_right_part) \
  item_left_part##item_right_part
#define STICK_ALTERNATIVE(item_left_part, item_right_part) \
  item_left_part%:%:item_right_part
```

```cpp
int main() {
  std::string hello_world_message = "Hello, World!";

  std::cout << "##   " << STICK_PRIMARY(hello_world, _message) << "\n";
  std::cout << "%:%: " << STICK_ALTERNATIVE(hello_world, _message) << std::endl;

  return 0;
}
```

We compile the test program by running the command:

Listing 49. Linux Terminal

```
g++ -o main main.cpp
```

then we launch it

Listing 50. Linux Terminal

```
./main
```

Example 11. The result of the execution that is displayed on the screen should be the following:

```
##   Hello, World!
%:%: Hello, World!
```

We execute the command,

Listing 51. Linux Terminal

```
echo $?
```

which outputs the result returned by the executable.

Example 12. The value should be:

```
0
```

2.5. Logically And

Logically And is used in complex conditions.

I'll show you how you can replace the basic and alternate variations of the logic and operator.

We create a folder in which to put the source code of the program.

Listing 52. Linux Terminal

```
mkdir -p ~/c++/sources/chapter_02_05_00/logically_and_01
```

Then we enter the newly created folder.

Listing 53. Linux Terminal

```
cd ~/c++/sources/chapter_02_05_00/logically_and_01
```

In this folder, we create the file main.cpp

Listing 54. Linux Terminal

```
code main.cpp
```

With the following content:

Listing 55. chapter_02_05_00/logically_and_01/main.cpp

```cpp
#include <bitset>
#include <ciso646>
#include <iomanip>
#include <iostream>
#include <sstream>

const std::string LEFT                    = "left";
```

```cpp
const std::string RIGHT                       = "right";
const std::string LEFT_PRIMARY_AND_RIGHT     = LEFT + " && " + RIGHT;
const std::string LEFT_ALTERNATIVE_AND_RIGHT = LEFT + " and " + RIGHT;

template <typename Operand_Type>
auto print(std::string const& operand_name, Operand_Type operand) {
  std::stringstream result;

  result << std::setw(LEFT_ALTERNATIVE_AND_RIGHT.length()) << operand_name
         << " = " << std::dec << std::setw(sizeof(operand) * 3) << +operand;
  result << ", 0x" << std::setfill('0') << std::setw(sizeof(operand) * 2)
         << std::uppercase << std::hex << +operand;
  result << ", 0b" << std::bitset<sizeof(operand) * 8>(operand) << "\n";

  return result;
}

typedef char Integer;

int main() {
  Integer left;
  Integer right;
  long long input;

  std::cout << "Please enter a \"" << LEFT << "\" operand:\n";
  std::cin >> input;
  left = static_cast<Integer>(input);
  std::cout << "and a \"" << RIGHT << "\" operand:\n";
  std::cin >> input;
  right = static_cast<Integer>(input);

  std::cout << std::endl;
  std::cout << print(LEFT, left).rdbuf();
  std::cout << print(RIGHT, right).rdbuf();
  std::cout << print(LEFT_PRIMARY_AND_RIGHT,
                     static_cast<Integer>(left && right))
                  .rdbuf();
  std::cout << print(LEFT_ALTERNATIVE_AND_RIGHT,
                     static_cast<Integer>(left and right))
                  .rdbuf();

  return EXIT_SUCCESS;
}
```

We compile the test program by running the command:

Listing 56. Linux Terminal

```
g++ -o main main.cpp
```

then we launch it

Listing 57. Linux Terminal

```
./main
```

Example 13. The result of the execution that is displayed on the screen should be the following:

```
Please enter a "left" operand:
and a "right" operand:

         left =  13, 0x0D, 0b00001101
        right =  27, 0x1B, 0b00011011
 left && right =   1, 0x01, 0b00000001
left and right =   1, 0x01, 0b00000001
```

We execute the command,

Listing 58. Linux Terminal

```
echo $?
```

which outputs the result returned by the executable.

Example 14. The value should be:

```
0
```

2.6. Bitwise And

Bitwise And is used in bitwise operations.

I'll show you how you can replace the basic and alternate variations of the bitwise and operator.

We create a folder in which to put the source code of the program.

Listing 59. Linux Terminal

```
mkdir -p ~/c++/sources/chapter_02_06_00/bitwise_and_01
```

Then we enter the newly created folder.

Listing 60. Linux Terminal

```
cd ~/c++/sources/chapter_02_06_00/bitwise_and_01
```

In this folder, we create the file main.cpp

Listing 61. Linux Terminal

```
code main.cpp
```

With the following content:

Listing 62. chapter_02_06_00/bitwise_and_01/main.cpp

```cpp
#include <bitset>
#include <ciso646>
#include <iomanip>
#include <iostream>
#include <sstream>

const std::string LEFT                        = "left";
```

```cpp
const std::string RIGHT                              = "right";
const std::string LEFT_PRIMARY_BITWISE_AND_RIGHT     = LEFT + " & " + RIGHT;
const std::string LEFT_ALTERNATIVE_BITWISE_AND_RIGHT = LEFT + " bitand " + RIGHT;

template <typename Operand_Type>
auto print(std::string const& operand_name, Operand_Type operand) {
  std::stringstream result;

  result << std::setw(LEFT_ALTERNATIVE_BITWISE_AND_RIGHT.length())
         << operand_name << " = " << std::dec << std::setw(sizeof(operand) * 3)
         << +operand;
  result << ", 0x" << std::setfill('0') << std::setw(sizeof(operand) * 2)
         << std::uppercase << std::hex << +operand;
  result << ", 0b" << std::bitset<sizeof(operand) * 8>(operand) << "\n";

  return result;
}

typedef char Integer;

int main() {
  Integer left;
  Integer right;
  long long input;

  std::cout << "Please enter a \"" << LEFT << "\" operand:\n";
  std::cin >> input;
  left = static_cast<Integer>(input);
  std::cout << "and a \"" << RIGHT << "\" operand:\n";
  std::cin >> input;
  right = static_cast<Integer>(input);

  std::cout << std::endl;
  std::cout << print(LEFT, left).rdbuf();
  std::cout << print(RIGHT, right).rdbuf();
  std::cout << print(LEFT_PRIMARY_BITWISE_AND_RIGHT,
                     static_cast<Integer>(left & right))
                   .rdbuf();
  std::cout << print(LEFT_ALTERNATIVE_BITWISE_AND_RIGHT,
                     static_cast<Integer>(left bitand right))
                   .rdbuf();

  return EXIT_SUCCESS;
}
```

We compile the test program by running the command:

Listing 63. Linux Terminal

```
g++ -o main main.cpp
```

then we launch it

Listing 64. Linux Terminal

```
./main
```

Example 15. The result of the execution that is displayed on the screen should be the following:

```
Please enter a "left" operand:
and a "right" operand:

            left =  13, 0x0D, 0b00001101
           right =  27, 0x1B, 0b00011011
    left & right =   9, 0x09, 0b00001001
left bitand right =   9, 0x09, 0b00001001
```

We execute the command,

Listing 65. Linux Terminal

```
echo $?
```

which outputs the result returned by the executable.

Example 16. The value should be:

```
0
```

2.7. Bitwise And With Acquisition

Bitwise And With Acquisition is used in bitwise operations.

I'll show you how you can replace the basic and alternate variations of the bitwise and with the acquisition operator.

We create a folder in which to put the source code of the program.

Listing 66. Linux Terminal

```
mkdir -p ~/c++/sources/chapter_02_07_00/bitwise_and_with_acquisition_01
```

Then we enter the newly created folder.

Listing 67. Linux Terminal

```
cd ~/c++/sources/chapter_02_07_00/bitwise_and_with_acquisition_01
```

In this folder, we create the file main.cpp

Listing 68. Linux Terminal

```
code main.cpp
```

With the following content:

Listing 69.
chapter_02_07_00/bitwise_and_with_acquisition_01/main.cpp

```cpp
#include <bitset>
#include <ciso646>
#include <iomanip>
#include <iostream>
#include <sstream>

const std::string LEFT                               = "left";
const std::string RIGHT                              = "right";
const std::string LEFT_PRIMARY_BITWISE_AND_RIGHT     = LEFT + " &= " + RIGHT;
const std::string LEFT_ALTERNATIVE_BITWISE_AND_RIGHT = LEFT + " and_eq " + RIGHT;

template <typename Operand_Type>
auto print(std::string const& operand_name, Operand_Type operand) {
  std::stringstream result;

  result << std::setw(LEFT_ALTERNATIVE_BITWISE_AND_RIGHT.length())
         << operand_name << " = " << std::dec << std::setw(sizeof(operand) * 3)
         << +operand;
  result << ", 0x" << std::setfill('0') << std::setw(sizeof(operand) * 2)
         << std::uppercase << std::hex << +operand;
  result << ", 0b" << std::bitset<sizeof(operand) * 8>(operand) << "\n";

  return result;
}

typedef char Integer;

int main() {
  Integer left;
  Integer right;
  long long input;

  std::cout << "Please enter a \"" << LEFT << "\" operand:\n";
  std::cin >> input;
  left = static_cast<Integer>(input);
  std::cout << "and a \"" << RIGHT << "\" operand:\n";
  std::cin >> input;
  right = static_cast<Integer>(input);

  std::cout << std::endl;
  std::cout << print(LEFT, left).rdbuf();
  std::cout << print(RIGHT, right).rdbuf();

  Integer result = left;
  result &= right;
  std::cout << print(LEFT_PRIMARY_BITWISE_AND_RIGHT, result).rdbuf();

  result = left;
```

```
    result and_eq right;
    std::cout << print(LEFT_ALTERNATIVE_BITWISE_AND_RIGHT, result).rdbuf();

    return EXIT_SUCCESS;
}
```

We compile the test program by running the command:

Listing 70. Linux Terminal

```
g++ -o main main.cpp
```

then we launch it

Listing 71. Linux Terminal

```
./main
```

Example 17. The result of the execution that is displayed on the screen should be the following:

```
Please enter a "left" operand:
and a "right" operand:

             left =  13, 0x0D, 0b00001101
            right =  27, 0x1B, 0b00011011
    left &= right =   9, 0x09, 0b00001001
left and_eq right =   9, 0x09, 0b00001001
```

We execute the command,

Listing 72. Linux Terminal

```
echo $?
```

which outputs the result returned by the

executable.

Example 18. The value should be:

```
0
```

2.8. Logically Or

Logically Or is used in complex conditions.

I'll show you how you can replace the basic and alternate variations of the logical or operator.

We create a folder in which to put the source code of the program.

Listing 73. Linux Terminal

```
mkdir -p ~/c++/sources/chapter_02_08_00/logically_or_01
```

Then we enter the newly created folder.

Listing 74. Linux Terminal

```
cd ~/c++/sources/chapter_02_08_00/logically_or_01
```

In this folder, we create the file main.cpp

Listing 75. Linux Terminal

```
code main.cpp
```

With the following content:

Listing 76. chapter_02_08_00/logically_or_01/main.cpp

```cpp
#include <bitset>
#include <ciso646>
#include <iomanip>
#include <iostream>
#include <sstream>

const std::string LEFT                 = "left";
```

```cpp
const std::string RIGHT                    = "right";
const std::string LEFT_PRIMARY_OR_RIGHT    = LEFT + " || " + RIGHT;
const std::string LEFT_ALTERNATIVE_OR_RIGHT = LEFT + " or " + RIGHT;

template <typename Operand_Type>
auto print(std::string const& operand_name, Operand_Type operand) {
  std::stringstream result;

  result << std::setw(LEFT_ALTERNATIVE_OR_RIGHT.length()) << operand_name
         << " = " << std::dec << std::setw(sizeof(operand) * 3) << +operand;
  result << ", 0x" << std::setfill('0') << std::setw(sizeof(operand) * 2)
         << std::uppercase << std::hex << +operand;
  result << ", 0b" << std::bitset<sizeof(operand) * 8>(operand) << "\n";

  return result;
}

typedef char Integer;

int main() {
  Integer left;
  Integer right;
  long long input;

  std::cout << "Please enter a \"" << LEFT << "\" operand:\n";
  std::cin >> input;
  left = static_cast<Integer>(input);
  std::cout << "and a \"" << RIGHT << "\" operand:\n";
  std::cin >> input;
  right = static_cast<Integer>(input);

  std::cout << std::endl;
  std::cout << print(LEFT, left).rdbuf();
  std::cout << print(RIGHT, right).rdbuf();
  std::cout << print(LEFT_PRIMARY_OR_RIGHT, static_cast<Integer>(left || right))
                   .rdbuf();
  std::cout << print(LEFT_ALTERNATIVE_OR_RIGHT,
                     static_cast<Integer>(left or right))
                   .rdbuf();

  return EXIT_SUCCESS;
}
```

We compile the test program by running the command:

Listing 77. Linux Terminal

```
g++ -o main main.cpp
```

then we launch it

Listing 78. Linux Terminal

```
./main
```

Example 19. The result of the execution that is displayed on the screen should be the following:

```
Please enter a "left" operand:
and a "right" operand:

          left =  13, 0x0D, 0b00001101
         right =  27, 0x1B, 0b00011011
left || right =   1, 0x01, 0b00000001
left or right =   1, 0x01, 0b00000001
```

We execute the command,

Listing 79. Linux Terminal

```
echo $?
```

which outputs the result returned by the executable.

Example 20. The value should be:

```
0
```

2.9. Bitwise Or

Bitwise Or is used in bitwise operations.

I'll show you how you can replace the basic and alternate variations of the bitwise or operator.

We create a folder in which to put the source code of the program.

Listing 80. Linux Terminal

```
mkdir -p ~/c++/sources/chapter_02_09_00/bitwise_or_01
```

Then we enter the newly created folder.

Listing 81. Linux Terminal

```
cd ~/c++/sources/chapter_02_09_00/bitwise_or_01
```

In this folder, we create the file main.cpp

Listing 82. Linux Terminal

```
code main.cpp
```

With the following content:

Listing 83. chapter_02_09_00/bitwise_or_01/main.cpp

```cpp
#include <bitset>
#include <ciso646>
#include <iomanip>
#include <iostream>
#include <sstream>

const std::string LEFT                    = "left";
```

```
const std::string RIGHT                             = "right";
const std::string LEFT_PRIMARY_BITWISE_OR_RIGHT     = LEFT + " | " + RIGHT;
const std::string LEFT_ALTERNATIVE_BITWISE_OR_RIGHT = LEFT + " bitor " + RIGHT;

template <typename Operand_Type>
auto print(std::string const& operand_name, Operand_Type operand) {
  std::stringstream result;

  result << std::setw(LEFT_ALTERNATIVE_BITWISE_OR_RIGHT.length())
         << operand_name << " = " << std::dec << std::setw(sizeof(operand) * 3)
         << +operand;
  result << ", 0x" << std::setfill('0') << std::setw(sizeof(operand) * 2)
         << std::uppercase << std::hex << +operand;
  result << ", 0b" << std::bitset<sizeof(operand) * 8>(operand) << "\n";

  return result;
}

typedef char Integer;

int main() {
  Integer left;
  Integer right;
  long long input;

  std::cout << "Please enter a \"" << LEFT << "\" operand:\n";
  std::cin >> input;
  left = static_cast<Integer>(input);
  std::cout << "and a \"" << RIGHT << "\" operand:\n";
  std::cin >> input;
  right = static_cast<Integer>(input);

  std::cout << std::endl;
  std::cout << print(LEFT, left).rdbuf();
  std::cout << print(RIGHT, right).rdbuf();
  std::cout << print(LEFT_PRIMARY_BITWISE_OR_RIGHT,
                     static_cast<Integer>(left | right))
                .rdbuf();
  std::cout << print(LEFT_ALTERNATIVE_BITWISE_OR_RIGHT,
                     static_cast<Integer>(left bitor right))
                .rdbuf();

  return EXIT_SUCCESS;
}
```

We compile the test program by running the command:

Listing 84. Linux Terminal

```
g++ -o main main.cpp
```

then we launch it

Listing 85. Linux Terminal

```
./main
```

Example 21. The result of the execution that is displayed on the screen should be the following:

```
Please enter a "left" operand:
and a "right" operand:

            left =  13, 0x0D, 0b00001101
           right =  27, 0x1B, 0b00011011
    left | right =  31, 0x1F, 0b00011111
left bitor right =  31, 0x1F, 0b00011111
```

We execute the command,

Listing 86. Linux Terminal

```
echo $?
```

which outputs the result returned by the executable.

Example 22. The value should be:

```
0
```

2.10. Bitwise Or With Acquisition

Bitwise Or With Acquisition is used in bitwise operations.

I'll show you how you can replace the basic and alternate variations of the bitwise or with the acquisition operator.

We create a folder in which to put the source code of the program.

Listing 87. Linux Terminal

```
mkdir -p ~/c++/sources/chapter_02_10_00/bitwise_or_with_acquisition_01
```

Then we enter the newly created folder.

Listing 88. Linux Terminal

```
cd ~/c++/sources/chapter_02_10_00/bitwise_or_with_acquisition_01
```

In this folder, we create the file main.cpp

Listing 89. Linux Terminal

```
code main.cpp
```

With the following content:

Listing 90.
chapter_02_10_00/bitwise_or_with_acquisition_01/main.cpp

```cpp
#include <bitset>
#include <ciso646>
#include <iomanip>
#include <iostream>
#include <sstream>

const std::string LEFT                          = "left";
const std::string RIGHT                         = "right";
const std::string LEFT_PRIMARY_BITWISE_OR_RIGHT     = LEFT + " |= " + RIGHT;
const std::string LEFT_ALTERNATIVE_BITWISE_OR_RIGHT = LEFT + " or_eq " + RIGHT;

template <typename Operand_Type>
auto print(std::string const& operand_name, Operand_Type operand) {
  std::stringstream result;

  result << std::setw(LEFT_ALTERNATIVE_BITWISE_OR_RIGHT.length())
         << operand_name << " = " << std::dec << std::setw(sizeof(operand) * 3)
         << +operand;
  result << ", 0x" << std::setfill('0') << std::setw(sizeof(operand) * 2)
         << std::uppercase << std::hex << +operand;
  result << ", 0b" << std::bitset<sizeof(operand) * 8>(operand) << "\n";

  return result;
}

typedef char Integer;

int main() {
  Integer left;
  Integer right;
  long long input;

  std::cout << "Please enter a \"" << LEFT << "\" operand:\n";
  std::cin >> input;
  left = static_cast<Integer>(input);
  std::cout << "and a \"" << RIGHT << "\" operand:\n";
  std::cin >> input;
  right = static_cast<Integer>(input);

  std::cout << std::endl;
  std::cout << print(LEFT, left).rdbuf();
  std::cout << print(RIGHT, right).rdbuf();

  Integer result = left;
  result |= right;
  std::cout << print(LEFT_PRIMARY_BITWISE_OR_RIGHT, result).rdbuf();

  result = left;
```

```
    result or_eq right;
    std::cout << print(LEFT_ALTERNATIVE_BITWISE_OR_RIGHT, result).rdbuf();

    return EXIT_SUCCESS;
}
```

We compile the test program by running the command:

Listing 91. Linux Terminal

```
g++ -o main main.cpp
```

then we launch it

Listing 92. Linux Terminal

```
./main
```

Example 23. The result of the execution that is displayed on the screen should be the following:

```
Please enter a "left" operand:
and a "right" operand:

            left =  13, 0x0D, 0b00001101
           right =  27, 0x1B, 0b00011011
   left |= right =  31, 0x1F, 0b00011111
left or_eq right =  31, 0x1F, 0b00011111
```

We execute the command,

Listing 93. Linux Terminal

```
echo $?
```

which outputs the result returned by the

executable.

Example 24. The value should be:

```
0
```

2.11. Bitwise Exclusionary Or

Bitwise Exclusionary Or is used in bitwise operations.

I'll show you how you can replace the basic and alternate variations of the bitwise exclusionary or operator.

We create a folder in which to put the source code of the program.

Listing 94. Linux Terminal

```
mkdir -p ~/c++/sources/chapter_02_11_00/bitwise_exclusionary_or_01
```

Then we enter the newly created folder.

Listing 95. Linux Terminal

```
cd ~/c++/sources/chapter_02_11_00/bitwise_exclusionary_or_01
```

In this folder, we create the file main.cpp

Listing 96. Linux Terminal

```
code main.cpp
```

With the following content:

Listing 97.
chapter_02_11_00/bitwise_exclusionary_or_01/main.cpp

```cpp
#include <bitset>
#include <ciso646>
#include <iomanip>
#include <iostream>
#include <sstream>

const std::string LEFT                                         = "left";
const std::string RIGHT                                        = "right";
const std::string LEFT_PRIMARY_BITWISE_EXCLUSIONARY_OR_RIGHT   = LEFT + " ^ " +
RIGHT;
const std::string LEFT_ALTERNATIVE_BITWISE_EXCLUSIONARY_OR_RIGHT = LEFT + " xor " +
RIGHT;

template <typename Operand_Type>
auto print(std::string const& operand_name, Operand_Type operand) {
  std::stringstream result;

  result << std::setw(LEFT_ALTERNATIVE_BITWISE_EXCLUSIONARY_OR_RIGHT.length())
         << operand_name << " = " << std::dec << std::setw(sizeof(operand) * 3)
         << +operand;
  result << ", 0x" << std::setfill('0') << std::setw(sizeof(operand) * 2)
         << std::uppercase << std::hex << +operand;
  result << ", 0b" << std::bitset<sizeof(operand) * 8>(operand) << "\n";

  return result;
}

typedef char Integer;

int main() {
  Integer left;
  Integer right;
  long long input;

  std::cout << "Please enter a \"" << LEFT << "\" operand:\n";
  std::cin >> input;
  left = static_cast<Integer>(input);
  std::cout << "and a \"" << RIGHT << "\" operand:\n";
  std::cin >> input;
  right = static_cast<Integer>(input);

  std::cout << std::endl;
  std::cout << print(LEFT, left).rdbuf();
  std::cout << print(RIGHT, right).rdbuf();
  std::cout << print(LEFT_PRIMARY_BITWISE_EXCLUSIONARY_OR_RIGHT,
                     static_cast<Integer>(left ^ right))
                     .rdbuf();
  std::cout << print(LEFT_ALTERNATIVE_BITWISE_EXCLUSIONARY_OR_RIGHT,
```

```
                static_cast<Integer>(left xor right))
                    .rdbuf();

    return EXIT_SUCCESS;
}
```

We compile the test program by running the command:

Listing 98. Linux Terminal

```
g++ -o main main.cpp
```

then we launch it

Listing 99. Linux Terminal

```
./main
```

Example 25. The result of the execution that is displayed on the screen should be the following:

```
Please enter a "left" operand:
and a "right" operand:

            left =  13, 0x0D, 0b00001101
           right =  27, 0x1B, 0b00011011
    left ^ right =  22, 0x16, 0b00010110
left xor right =  22, 0x16, 0b00010110
```

We execute the command,

Listing 100. Linux Terminal

```
echo $?
```

which outputs the result returned by the

executable.

Example 26. The value should be:

```
0
```

2.12. Bitwise Exclusionary Or With Acquisition

Bitwise Or With Acquisition is used in bitwise operations.

I'll show you how you can replace the basic and alternate variations of the bitwise or with the acquisition operator.

We create a folder in which to put the source code of the program.

Listing 101. Linux Terminal

```
mkdir -p ~/c++/sources/chapter_02_12_00/bitwise_exclusionary_or_with_acquisition_01
```

Then we enter the newly created folder.

Listing 102. Linux Terminal

```
cd ~/c++/sources/chapter_02_12_00/bitwise_exclusionary_or_with_acquisition_01
```

In this folder, we create the file `main.cpp`

Listing 103. Linux Terminal

```
code main.cpp
```

With the following content:

Listing 104.
chapter_02_12_00/bitwise_exclusionary_or_with_acquisition
_01/main.cpp

```cpp
#include <bitset>
#include <ciso646>
#include <iomanip>
#include <iostream>
#include <sstream>

const std::string LEFT                                          = "left";
const std::string RIGHT                                         = "right";
const std::string LEFT_PRIMARY_BITWISE_EXCLUSIONARY_OR_RIGHT     = LEFT + " ^= " +
RIGHT;
const std::string LEFT_ALTERNATIVE_BITWISE_EXCLUSIONARY_OR_RIGHT = LEFT + " xor_eq
" + RIGHT;

template <typename Operand_Type>
auto print(std::string const& operand_name, Operand_Type operand) {
  std::stringstream result;

  result << std::setw(LEFT_ALTERNATIVE_BITWISE_EXCLUSIONARY_OR_RIGHT.length())
         << operand_name << " = " << std::dec << std::setw(sizeof(operand) * 3)
         << +operand;
  result << ", 0x" << std::setfill('0') << std::setw(sizeof(operand) * 2)
         << std::uppercase << std::hex << +operand;
  result << ", 0b" << std::bitset<sizeof(operand) * 8>(operand) << "\n";

  return result;
}

typedef char Integer;

int main() {
  Integer left;
  Integer right;
  long long input;

  std::cout << "Please enter a \"" << LEFT << "\" operand:\n";
  std::cin >> input;
  left = static_cast<Integer>(input);
  std::cout << "and a \"" << RIGHT << "\" operand:\n";
  std::cin >> input;
  right = static_cast<Integer>(input);

  std::cout << std::endl;
  std::cout << print(LEFT, left).rdbuf();
  std::cout << print(RIGHT, right).rdbuf();

  Integer result = left;
```

```
    result ^= right;
    std::cout
        << print(LEFT_PRIMARY_BITWISE_EXCLUSIONARY_OR_RIGHT, result).rdbuf();

    result = left;
    result xor_eq right;
    std::cout
        << print(LEFT_ALTERNATIVE_BITWISE_EXCLUSIONARY_OR_RIGHT, result).rdbuf();

    return EXIT_SUCCESS;
}
```

We compile the test program by running the command:

Listing 105. Linux Terminal

```
g++ -o main main.cpp
```

then we launch it

Listing 106. Linux Terminal

```
./main
```

Example 27. The result of the execution that is displayed on the screen should be the following:

```
Please enter a "left" operand:
and a "right" operand:

             left =  13, 0x0D, 0b00001101
            right =  27, 0x1B, 0b00011011
    left ^= right =  22, 0x16, 0b00010110
left xor_eq right =  22, 0x16, 0b00010110
```

We execute the command,

Listing 107. Linux Terminal

```
echo $?
```

which outputs the result returned by the executable.

Example 28. The value should be:

```
0
```

2.13. Logical Negation

Logical Negation is used in conditions.

I'll show you how you can replace the basic and alternate variations of the logical negation operator.

We create a folder in which to put the source code of the program.

Listing 108. Linux Terminal

```
mkdir -p ~/c++/sources/chapter_02_13_00/logical_negation_01
```

Then we enter the newly created folder.

Listing 109. Linux Terminal

```
cd ~/c++/sources/chapter_02_13_00/logical_negation_01
```

In this folder, we create the file main.cpp

Listing 110. Linux Terminal

```
code main.cpp
```

With the following content:

Listing 111. chapter_02_13_00/logical_negation_01/main.cpp

```cpp
#include <bitset>
#include <ciso646>
#include <iomanip>
#include <iostream>
#include <sstream>
```

```cpp
st std::string LEFT                                    = "left";
nst std::string RIGHT                                  = "right";
const std::string LEFT_PRIMARY_LOGICAL_NEGATION_RIGHT     = "!" + RIGHT;
const std::string LEFT_ALTERNATIVE_LOGICAL_NEGATION_RIGHT = "not " + RIGHT;

template <typename Operand_Type>
auto print(std::string const& operand_name, Operand_Type operand) {
  std::stringstream result;

  result << std::setw(LEFT_ALTERNATIVE_LOGICAL_NEGATION_RIGHT.length())
         << operand_name << " = " << std::dec << std::setw(sizeof(operand) * 3)
         << +operand;
  result << ", 0x" << std::setfill('0') << std::setw(sizeof(operand) * 2)
         << std::uppercase << std::hex << +operand;
  result << ", 0b" << std::bitset<sizeof(operand) * 8>(operand) << "\n";

  return result;
}

typedef char Integer;

int main() {
  Integer right;
  long long input;

  std::cout << "Please enter a \"" << RIGHT << "\" operand:\n";
  std::cin >> input;
  right = static_cast<Integer>(input);

  std::cout << std::endl;
  std::cout << print(RIGHT, right).rdbuf();
  std::cout << print(LEFT_PRIMARY_LOGICAL_NEGATION_RIGHT,
                     static_cast<Integer>(!right))
                  .rdbuf();
  std::cout << print(LEFT_ALTERNATIVE_LOGICAL_NEGATION_RIGHT,
                     static_cast<Integer>(not right))
                  .rdbuf();

  return EXIT_SUCCESS;
}
```

We compile the test program by running the command:

Listing 112. Linux Terminal

```
g++ -o main main.cpp
```

then we launch it

Listing 113. Linux Terminal

```
./main
```

Example 29. The result of the execution that is displayed on the screen should be the following:

```
Please enter a "right" operand:

     right =  13, 0x0D, 0b00001101
    !right =   0, 0x00, 0b00000000
 not right =   0, 0x00, 0b00000000
```

We execute the command,

Listing 114. Linux Terminal

```
echo $?
```

which outputs the result returned by the executable.

Example 30. The value should be:

```
0
```

2.14. Logical Negation With Acquisition

Logical Negation With Acquisition is used in conditions.

I'll show you how you can replace the basic and alternate variations of the logical negation with the acquisition operator.

We create a folder in which to put the source code of the program.

Listing 115. Linux Terminal

```
mkdir -p ~/c++/sources/chapter_02_14_00/logical_negation_with_acquisition_01
```

Then we enter the newly created folder.

Listing 116. Linux Terminal

```
cd ~/c++/sources/chapter_02_14_00/logical_negation_with_acquisition_01
```

In this folder, we create the file main.cpp

Listing 117. Linux Terminal

```
code main.cpp
```

With the following content:

Listing 118.
chapter_02_14_00/logical_negation_with_acquisition_01/mai
n.cpp

```cpp
#include <bitset>
#include <ciso646>
#include <iomanip>
#include <iostream>
#include <sstream>

const std::string LEFT                                = "left";
const std::string RIGHT                               = "right";
const std::string LEFT_PRIMARY_LOGICAL_NEGATION_RIGHT     = LEFT + "!=" + RIGHT;
const std::string LEFT_ALTERNATIVE_LOGICAL_NEGATION_RIGHT = LEFT + " not_eq " +
RIGHT;

template <typename Operand_Type>
auto print(std::string const& operand_name, Operand_Type operand) {
  std::stringstream result;

  result << std::setw(LEFT_ALTERNATIVE_LOGICAL_NEGATION_RIGHT.length())
         << operand_name << " = " << std::dec << std::setw(sizeof(operand) * 3)
         << +operand;
  result << ", 0x" << std::setfill('0') << std::setw(sizeof(operand) * 2)
         << std::uppercase << std::hex << +operand;
  result << ", 0b" << std::bitset<sizeof(operand) * 8>(operand) << "\n";

  return result;
}

typedef char Integer;

int main() {
  Integer left;
  Integer right;
  long long input;

  std::cout << "Please enter a \"" << LEFT << "\" operand:\n";
  std::cin >> input;
  left = static_cast<Integer>(input);
  std::cout << "and a \"" << RIGHT << "\" operand:\n";
  std::cin >> input;
  right = static_cast<Integer>(input);

  std::cout << std::endl;
  std::cout << print(LEFT, left).rdbuf();
  std::cout << print(RIGHT, right).rdbuf();
  std::cout << print(LEFT_PRIMARY_LOGICAL_NEGATION_RIGHT,
                     static_cast<Integer>(left != right))
                  .rdbuf();
```

```
  std::cout << print(LEFT_ALTERNATIVE_LOGICAL_NEGATION_RIGHT,
                static_cast<Integer>(left not_eq right))
              .rdbuf();

  return EXIT_SUCCESS;
}
```

We compile the test program by running the command:

Listing 119. Linux Terminal

```
g++ -o main main.cpp
```

then we launch it

Listing 120. Linux Terminal

```
./main
```

Example 31. The result of the execution that is displayed on the screen should be the following:

```
Please enter a "left" operand:
and a "right" operand:

              left =  13, 0x0D, 0b00001101
             right =  27, 0x1B, 0b00011011
       left!=right =   1, 0x01, 0b00000001
 left not_eq right =   1, 0x01, 0b00000001
```

We execute the command,

Listing 121. Linux Terminal

```
echo $?
```

which outputs the result returned by the

executable.

Example 32. The value should be:

```
0
```

2.15. Bitwise Compliment

Bitwise Compliment is used in bitwise operations.

I'll show you how you can replace the basic and alternate variations of the bitwise complement operator.

We create a folder in which to put the source code of the program.

Listing 122. Linux Terminal

```
mkdir -p ~/c++/sources/chapter_02_15_00/bitwise_compliment_01
```

Then we enter the newly created folder.

Listing 123. Linux Terminal

```
cd ~/c++/sources/chapter_02_15_00/bitwise_compliment_01
```

In this folder, we create the file main.cpp

Listing 124. Linux Terminal

```
code main.cpp
```

With the following content:

Listing 125.
chapter_02_15_00/bitwise_compliment_01/main.cpp

```
#include <bitset>
#include <ciso646>
```

```cpp
#include <iomanip>
#include <iostream>
#include <sstream>

const std::string RIGHT                                  = "right";
const std::string LEFT_PRIMARY_BITWISE_COMPLIMENT_RIGHT     = "~" + RIGHT;
const std::string LEFT_ALTERNATIVE_BITWISE_COMPLIMENT_RIGHT = "compl " + RIGHT;

template <typename Operand_Type>
auto print(std::string const& operand_name, Operand_Type operand) {
  std::stringstream result;

  result << std::setw(LEFT_ALTERNATIVE_BITWISE_COMPLIMENT_RIGHT.length()) //
         << operand_name                                                  //
         << " = "                                                         //
         << std::dec                                                      //
         << std::setw(sizeof(operand) * 3)                                //
         << +operand;                                                     //
  result << ", 0x"                                                        //
         << std::setfill('0')                                            //
         << std::setw(sizeof(operand) * 2)                                //
         << std::uppercase                                                //
         << std::hex                                                      //
         << +operand;                                                     //
  result << ", 0b"                                                        //
         << std::bitset<sizeof(operand) * 8>(operand)                     //
         << "\n";                                                         //

  return result;
}

class Primary_Compliment_Class {
 public:
  Primary_Compliment_Class() {
    std::cout << "Primary_Compliment_Class constructor\n";
  }
  ~Primary_Compliment_Class() {
    std::cout << "~Primary_Compliment_Class destructor\n";
  }
};

class Alternative_Compliment_Class {
 public:
  Alternative_Compliment_Class() {
    std::cout << "Alternative_Compliment_Class constructor\n";
  }
  compl Alternative_Compliment_Class() {
    std::cout << "compl Alternative_Compliment_Class destructor\n";
  }
};

struct Primary_Compliment_Structure {
```

```cpp
  Primary_Compliment_Structure() {
    std::cout << "Primary_Compliment_Structure constructor\n";
  }
  ~Primary_Compliment_Structure() {
    std::cout << "~Primary_Compliment_Structure destructor\n";
  }
};

struct Alternative_Compliment_Structure {
  Alternative_Compliment_Structure() {
    std::cout << "Alternative_Compliment_Structure constructor\n";
  }
  compl Alternative_Compliment_Structure() {
    std::cout << "compl Alternative_Compliment_Structure destructor\n";
  }
};

typedef char Integer;

int main() {
  Primary_Compliment_Class primary_compliment_class;
  Alternative_Compliment_Class alternative_compliment_class;
  Primary_Compliment_Structure primary_compliment_structure;
  Alternative_Compliment_Structure alternative_compliment_structure;

  Integer right;
  long long input;

  std::cout << "\nPlease enter a \"" << RIGHT << "\" operand:\n";
  std::cin >> input;
  right = static_cast<Integer>(input);

  std::cout << std::endl;
  std::cout << print(RIGHT, right).rdbuf();
  std::cout << print(LEFT_PRIMARY_BITWISE_COMPLIMENT_RIGHT,
                     static_cast<Integer>(~right))
                  .rdbuf();
  std::cout << print(LEFT_ALTERNATIVE_BITWISE_COMPLIMENT_RIGHT,
                     static_cast<Integer>(compl right))
                  .rdbuf();

  std::cout << std::endl;

  return EXIT_SUCCESS;
}
```

We compile the test program by running the command:

Listing 126. Linux Terminal

```
g++ -o main main.cpp
```

then we launch it

Listing 127. Linux Terminal

```
./main
```

Example 33. The result of the execution that is displayed on the screen should be the following:

```
Primary_Compliment_Class constructor
Alternative_Compliment_Class constructor
Primary_Compliment_Structure constructor
Alternative_Compliment_Structure constructor

Please enter a "right" operand:

      right =  13, 0x0D, 0b00001101
     ~right = -14, 0xFFFFFFF2, 0b11110010
compl right = -14, 0xFFFFFFF2, 0b11110010

compl Alternative_Compliment_Structure destructor
~Primary_Compliment_Structure destructor
compl Alternative_Compliment_Class destructor
~Primary_Compliment_Class destructor
```

We execute the command,

Listing 128. Linux Terminal

```
echo $?
```

which outputs the result returned by the executable.

Example 34. The value should be:

```
0
```

Chapter 3. Comments

We use comments to describe in human-readable language what a piece of code is for. We can also use them to exclude a part of the program code that is not completely ready at the moment or is temporarily not needed by us.

Primary usage	Comment type	Description
`// commented text`	comment to the end of current line	Ignores all to the end of line

`/*`
`commented text`
`...`
`*/`
	multiline comment	Comments all between start `/*` and end `*/` of this type of comment

`#if 0`
`commented text`
`...`
`#endif`
	multiline preprocessing comment - #if 0	Comments all lines between `#if 0` and `#endif` of this type of comment

`#ifdef COMMENT`
`commented text`
`...`
`#endif`
	multiline preprocessing comment - #ifdef COMMENT	Comments all lines between `#ifdef COMMENT` and `#endif` if COMMENT is not already defined with preprocessing `#define` directive

In the following sections, I will show examples of different types of **C++** comments.

3.1. Comment To The End of The Current Line

I'll show you how you can comment to the end of the line.

We create a folder in which to put the source code of the program.

Listing 129. Linux Terminal

```
mkdir -p ~/c++/sources/chapter_03_01_00/comment_to_the_end_of_line_01
```

Then we enter the newly created folder.

Listing 130. Linux Terminal

```
cd ~/c++/sources/chapter_03_01_00/comment_to_the_end_of_line_01
```

In this folder, we create the file main.cpp

Listing 131. Linux Terminal

```
code main.cpp
```

With the following content:

Listing 132.
chapter_03_01_00/comment_to_the_end_of_line_01/main.cpp

```cpp
#include <cstdlib>    // <-- EXIT_SUCCESS
#include <iostream>   // <-- std::cout, <<, std::endl

namespace comments {

void print_message(std::string message) {
```

```
  // Output message to the console:
  std::cout << message << std::endl;
}

} // namespace comments
using namespace comments;

// Following function `main` is an entry point to the C++ program:
int main() {
  print_message("Hello from comment to the end of current line '//'");

  // Exiting with the success status --> `0`:
  return EXIT_SUCCESS;
}
```

We compile the test program by running the command:

Listing 133. Linux Terminal

```
g++ -o main main.cpp
```

then we launch it

Listing 134. Linux Terminal

```
./main
```

Example 35. The result of the execution that is displayed on the screen should be the following:

```
Hello from comment to the end of current line '//'
```

We execute the command,

Listing 135. Linux Terminal

```
echo $?
```

which outputs the result returned by the executable.

Example 36. The value should be:

```
0
```

3.2. Multiline Comment

I'll show you how you can use a multiline comment.

We create a folder in which to put the source code of the program.

Listing 136. Linux Terminal

```
mkdir -p ~/c++/sources/chapter_03_02_00/multiline_comment_01
```

Then we enter the newly created folder.

Listing 137. Linux Terminal

```
cd ~/c++/sources/chapter_03_02_00/multiline_comment_01
```

In this folder, we create the file main.cpp

Listing 138. Linux Terminal

```
code main.cpp
```

With the following content:

Listing 139. chapter_03_02_00/multiline_comment_01/main.cpp

```cpp
#include <cstdlib>  /* <-- EXIT_SUCCESS */
#include <iostream> /* <-- std::cout, <<, std::endln */

namespace comments {

void print_message(std::string message) {
  /*
   Output message
   to the console:
   */
  std::cout << message << std::endl;
}

} // namespace comments
using namespace comments;

/*
 Following function `main`
 is an entry point to the C++ program:
 */
int main() {
  print_message("Hello from the multiline comment '/* ... */'");

  /*
   Exiting with the success status --> `0`:
   */
  return EXIT_SUCCESS;
}
```

We compile the test program by running the command:

Listing 140. Linux Terminal

```
g++ -o main main.cpp
```

then we launch it

Listing 141. Linux Terminal

```
./main
```

Example 37. The result of the execution that is displayed on the screen should be the following:

```
Hello from the multiline comment '/* ... */'
```

We execute the command,

Listing 142. Linux Terminal

```
echo $?
```

which outputs the result returned by the executable.

Example 38. The value should be:

```
0
```

3.3. Multiline Preprocessing Comment

I'll show you how you can use a multiline preprocessing comment.

We create a folder in which to put the source code of the program.

Listing 143. Linux Terminal

```
mkdir -p ~/c++/sources/chapter_03_03_00/multiline_preprocessing_comment_01
```

Then we enter the newly created folder.

Listing 144. Linux Terminal

```
cd ~/c++/sources/chapter_03_03_00/multiline_preprocessing_comment_01
```

In this folder, we create the file `main.cpp`

Listing 145. Linux Terminal

```
code main.cpp
```

With the following content:

Listing 146.
`chapter_03_03_00/multiline_preprocessing_comment_01/main.cpp`

```cpp
#include <cstdlib>   // <-- EXIT_SUCCESS
#include <iostream>  // <-- std::cout, <<, std::endl

#if 0

namespace comments {

void print_message(std::string message) {
  // Output message to the console:
  std::cout << message << std::endl;
}

} // namespace comments
using namespace comments;

#endif // 0

#ifdef COMMENT

namespace comments {

void print_message(const char* message) {
  // Output message to the console:
  std::cout << message << std::endl;
}

} // namespace comments
```

```cpp
using namespace comments;

#endif  // COMMENT

void print_message(std::string const& message) {
  // Output message to the console:
  std::cout << message << std::endl;
}

/*
 Following function `main`
 is an entry point to the C++ program:
*/
int main() {
  print_message("Hello from the multiline preprocessing comment");

  // Exiting with the success status --> `0`:
  return EXIT_SUCCESS;
}
```

We compile the test program by running the command:

Listing 147. Linux Terminal

```
g++ -o main main.cpp
```

then we launch it

Listing 148. Linux Terminal

```
./main
```

Example 39. The result of the execution that is displayed on the screen should be the following:

```
Hello from the multiline preprocessing comment
```

We execute the command,

Listing 149. Linux Terminal

```
echo $?
```

which outputs the result returned by the executable.

Example 40. The value should be:

```
0
```

Chapter 4. Description of the program code

4.1. square_brackets_01 / main.cpp

Listing 150. ~/c++/sources/chapter_02_01_00/square_brackets_01/main.cpp

```cpp
#include <array>
#include <iostream>

int main() {
  std::array<int, 3> int_array{1, 2, 3};

  std::cout << "Primary square brackets '[ ... ]'\n";
  for (int index = 0, size = int_array.size(); index < size; ++index) {
    std::cout << "int_array[ " << index << " ] = ";
    std::cout << int_array[index] << "\n";
  }
  std::cout << "\n";

  std::cout << "Alternative square brackets '<: ... :>'\n";
  for (int index = 0, size = int_array.size(); index < size; ++index) {
    std::cout << "int_array<: " << index << " :> = ";
    std::cout << int_array <: index :> << "\n";
  }
  std::cout << "\n";

  std::cout << "Open primary, close alternative square brackets '[ ... :>'\n";
  for (int index = 0, size = int_array.size(); index < size; ++index) {
    std::cout << "int_array[ " << index << " :> = ";
    std::cout << int_array[index:> << "\n";
  }
  std::cout << "\n";

  std::cout << "Open alternative, close primary square brackets '<: ... ]'\n";
  for (int index = 0, size = int_array.size(); index < size; ++index) {
    std::cout << "int_array<: " << index << " ] = ";
    std::cout << int_array<:index] << "\n";
  }
  std::cout << std::endl;

  return EXIT_SUCCESS;
}
```

The above listing is the entire code of the example program that shows the practical use of the alternate <: :> and basic [ ] square brackets in **C++**. Below I will briefly explain the individual parts of this source code. ---

Listing 151. `main.cpp#1`

```
1 #include <array>
```

Load definition of the `array` **C++ Standard Template Library (STL)** data structure

The `array` structure represents a sequence of indexed elements that can be accessed instantly by specifying their index. The size of this structure cannot be dynamically resized after declaration, and access to its elements is more efficient than the vector structure, which can be dynamically resized.

Listing 152. `main.cpp#2`

```
2 #include <iostream>
```

The `include` preprocessing loads **C++** definitions for Input/Output (I/O) operations with streams.

In our program we use only:

- `std::cout` → output stream,
- `<<` → send right operand to the output stream (left operand) and

- std::endl → **send** new line to the output stream and flushes stream content.

Listing 153. main.cpp#4

```
4 int main() {
```

Declaration of entry point for our **C++** program → function main which returns an integer value and in this case it declared without arguments. From here starting execution of our program. The function main can receive some input parameters like number of command line arguments and an array with the arguments itself.

Like:

```
int main(int arguments_count, char* arguments[]) { ... return 0; }
```

or

```
int main(int arguments_count, char** arguments) { ... return 0; }
```

Listing 154. main.cpp#5

```
5   std::array<int, 3> int_array{1, 2, 3};
```

Explicit declaration of constant length array

with integers.

Listing 155. Also we can use implicit type and size initialization like this:

```
std::array int_array{1, 2, 3};
```

Listing 156. main.cpp#7..12

```
 7    std::cout << "Primary square brackets '[ ... ]'\n";
 8    for (int index = 0, size = int_array.size(); index < size; ++index) {
 9      std::cout << "int_array[ " << index << " ] = ";
10      std::cout << int_array[index] << "\n";
11    }
12    std::cout << "\n";
```

Printing in the loop the array items using primary square brackets [ ]. The line before the loop just prints a message. Line after loop prints an empty new line.

Listing 157. We use loop for *with the following structure:*

```
for(<initialization>; <loop condition>; <loop parameters changing>) {
    <loop body>
}
```

Listing 158. main.cpp#14..19

```
14    std::cout << "Alternative square brackets '<: ... :>'\n";
15    for (int index = 0, size = int_array.size(); index < size; ++index) {
16      std::cout << "int_array<: " << index << " :> = ";
17      std::cout << int_array <: index :> << "\n";
18    }
19    std::cout << "\n";
```

Printing in the loop the array items using alternative square brackets <: :>.

```
21   std::cout << "Open primary, close alternative square brackets '[ ... :>'\n";
22   for (int index = 0, size = int_array.size(); index < size; ++index) {
23     std::cout << "int_array[ " << index << " :> = ";
24     std::cout << int_array[index:> << "\n";
25   }
26   std::cout << "\n";
```

Printing in the loop the array items using open primary [and close alternative :> square brackets.

Listing 160. main.cpp#28..33

```
28   std::cout << "Open alternative, close primary square brackets '<: ... ]'\n";
29   for (int index = 0, size = int_array.size(); index < size; ++index) {
30     std::cout << "int_array<: " << index << " ] = ";
31     std::cout << int_array<:index] << "\n";
32   }
33   std::cout << std::endl;
```

Printing in the loop the array items using open alternative <: and close primary] square brackets.

Listing 161. main.cpp#35

```
35   return EXIT_SUCCESS;
```

At this line, the main function returns an EXIT_SUCCESS preprocessing definition whose value is 0. Normally this means that the program exits successfully.

Listing 162. `main.cpp#36`

```
36 }
```

This is the end of the `main` function body and here all variables must be destroyed. The wonderful **Resource Acquisition Is Initialization (RAII)** is in action → inside the figure brackets block for any class object, variable, or constant declaration constructor is called and when exiting from such block the destructor is called and all `stack` variables are destroyed automatically. With this functionality, we can allocate and release any type of resources like → memory, files, connections, mutexes, database resources, and many more.

4.2. figure_brackets_01 / main.cpp

Listing 163. ~/c++/sources/chapter_02_02_00/figure_brackets_01/main.cpp

```cpp
1  #include <cstdlib>   // EXIT_SUCCESS
2  #include <cstring>   // strchr
3  #include <iostream>  // std::cout, <<, std::endl
4  #include <typeinfo>  // typeid
5
6  //
7  // primary namespace braces
8  //
9  namespace curly_braces {
10
11  // function definitions
12  void primary_function_definition() {
13    std::cout << __FUNCTION__ << "( ... ) { ... }\n";
14  }
15  void alternative_function_definition() <%
16    std::cout << __FUNCTION__ << "( ... ) <% ... %>\n";
17  %>
18
19  } // namespace curly_braces
20  using namespace curly_braces;
21
22  //
23  // alternative namespace braces
24  //
25  namespace helpers <%
26
27  std::string remove_leading_numbers(std::string const& value) {
28    size_t index = 0;
29
30    if (value.length() > 0) {
31      while (strchr("0123456789", value.at(index)) != nullptr) {
32        ++index;
33      }
34    }
35
36    std::string result = value.substr(index);
37
38    return result;
39  } // namespace std::stringremove_leading_numbers(std::stringconst&value)
40
41  %> // namespace helpers
```

```cpp
42  using namespace helpers;
43
44  // class definitions:
45  class Primary_Figure_Brackets_Class_Definition {
46   public:
47    Primary_Figure_Brackets_Class_Definition() {
48      std::cout << remove_leading_numbers(typeid(*this).name()) << " { ... };\n";
49    }
50  };
51  class Alternative_Figure_Brackets_Class_Definition <%
52   public:
53    Alternative_Figure_Brackets_Class_Definition() {
54      std::cout << remove_leading_numbers(typeid(*this).name()) << " <% ... %>;
    \n";
55    }
56  %>;
57
58  // structure definitions:
59  struct Primary_Figure_Brackets_Structure_Definition {
60    Primary_Figure_Brackets_Structure_Definition() {
61      std::cout << remove_leading_numbers(typeid(*this).name()) << " { ... };\n";
62    }
63  };
64  struct Alternative_Figure_Brackets_Structure_Definition <%
65    Alternative_Figure_Brackets_Structure_Definition() {
66      std::cout << remove_leading_numbers(typeid(*this).name()) << " <% ... %>;
    \n";
67    }
68  %>;
69
70  int main() {
71    primary_function_definition();
72    alternative_function_definition();
73    std::cout << "\n";
74
75    const Primary_Figure_Brackets_Class_Definition
76        primary_figure_brackets_class_definition;
77    const Alternative_Figure_Brackets_Class_Definition
78        alternative_figure_brackets_class_definition;
79    Primary_Figure_Brackets_Structure_Definition
80        primary_figure_brackets_structure_definition;
81    Alternative_Figure_Brackets_Structure_Definition
82        alternative_figure_brackets_structure_definition;
83    std::cout << "\n";
84
85    int number = 10;
86
87    std::cout << "Primary figure brackets '{ " << number << " }'\n";
88
89    <%
90      int number = 20;
91
```

```cpp
 92    std::cout << "Alternative figure brackets ";
 93    std::cout << "'<% ";
 94    std::cout << number;
 95    std::cout << " %>'\n";
 96  %>
 97
 98  {
 99    int number = 30;
100
101    std::cout << "Primary open, alternative close figure brackets ";
102    std::cout << "'{ ";
103    std::cout << number;
104    std::cout << " %>'\n";
105  %>
106
107  <%
108    int number = 40;
109
110    std::cout << "Alternative open, primary close figure brackets ";
111    std::cout << "'<% ";
112    std::cout << number;
113    std::cout << " }'\n";
114  }
115
116  std::cout << "Primary figure brackets '{ " << number << " }'\n\n";
117
118  // constant initialization:
119  const int primary_initialized_integer_constant{1};
120  std::cout << "primary_initialized_integer_constant{ "
121            << primary_initialized_integer_constant << " }\n";
122  const int alternative_initialized_integer_constant<% 2 %>;
123  std::cout << "alternative_initialized_integer_constant<% "
124            << alternative_initialized_integer_constant << " %>\n\n";
125
126  // variable initialization:
127  int primary_initialized_integer_variable{3};
128  std::cout << "primary_initialized_integer_variable{ "
129            << primary_initialized_integer_variable << " }\n";
130  int alternative_initialized_integer_variable<% 4 %>;
131  std::cout << "alternative_initialized_integer_variable<% "
132            << alternative_initialized_integer_variable << " %>" << std::endl;
133
134  return EXIT_SUCCESS;
135 }
```

The above code contains examples that demonstrate the use of the basic { } and alternative <% %> curly brace operators in **C++**.

Listing 164. main.cpp#1

```
1 #include <cstdlib>   // EXIT_SUCCESS
```

The include preprocessor directive loads standard C language definitions in our program we use only EXIT_SUCCESS preprocessing definition whose value is 0.

Listing 165. main.cpp#2

```
2 #include <cstring>   // strchr
```

This row loads **C** language functions in the **C++** regarding string manipulations. In this program we use only strchr function the character as the second argument is contained in the string (char array) passed as the first argument.

Listing 166. main.cpp#3

```
3 #include <iostream>  // std::cout, <<, std::endl
```

The include preprocessing loads **C++** definitions for Input/Output (I/O) operations with streams.

In our program we use only:

- std::cout → output stream,

- `<<` → send right operand to the output stream (left operand) and

- `std::endl` → send new line to the output stream and flushes stream content.

Listing 167. main.cpp#4

```
4 #include <typeinfo>  // typeid
```

Including the type information definitions, in this case, we use only typeid.

Listing 168. main.cpp#6..8

```
6 //
7 // primary namespace braces
8 //
```

Comment describing the following namespace braces type.

Listing 169. main.cpp#9..20

```
 9 namespace curly_braces {
10
11 // function definitions
12 void primary_function_definition() {
13   std::cout << __FUNCTION__ << "( ... ) { ... }\n";
14 }
15 void alternative_function_definition() <%
16   std::cout << __FUNCTION__ << "( ... ) <% ... %>\n";
17 %>
18
19 } // namespace curly_braces
```

```
20 using namespace curly_braces;
```

Namespace with figure braces, containing two functions one of them with primary braces { } and another one with alternative braces <% %>.

Listing 170. `main.cpp#22..42`

```
22 //
23 // alternative namespace braces
24 //
25 namespace helpers <%
26
27 std::string remove_leading_numbers(std::string const& value) {
28   size_t index = 0;
29
30   if (value.length() > 0) {
31     while (strchr("0123456789", value.at(index)) != nullptr) {
32       ++index;
33     }
34   }
35
36   std::string result = value.substr(index);
37
38   return result;
39 } // namespace std::stringremove_leading_numbers(std::stringconst&value)
40
41 %> // namespace helpers
42 using namespace helpers;
```

Namespace with alternative figure braces <% %>, containing a function that gets a string value with leading numbers and returns the same string without leading numbers. The function uses **C++** condition operator `if` and pre-condition loop `while`

You can experiment with this function by calling

it with different parameters, changing its conditions, and debugging it, as described in Section 1.2.1

Listing 171. main.cpp#44..56

```
44 // class definitions:
45 class Primary_Figure_Brackets_Class_Definition {
46   public:
47     Primary_Figure_Brackets_Class_Definition() {
48       std::cout << remove_leading_numbers(typeid(*this).name()) << " { ... };\n";
49     }
50 };
51 class Alternative_Figure_Brackets_Class_Definition <%
52   public:
53     Alternative_Figure_Brackets_Class_Definition() {
54       std::cout << remove_leading_numbers(typeid(*this).name()) << " <% ... %>;\n";
55     }
56 %>;
```

This code contains two classes with its constructors. Every constructor prints its class name using typeid C++ function and our function for removing leading numbers. One of the classes is declared by using primary figure braces and another with alternative figure braces.

Listing 172. main.cpp#59..68

```
59 struct Primary_Figure_Brackets_Structure_Definition {
60   Primary_Figure_Brackets_Structure_Definition() {
61     std::cout << remove_leading_numbers(typeid(*this).name()) << " { ... };\n";
62   }
63 };
64 struct Alternative_Figure_Brackets_Structure_Definition <%
```

```
65   Alternative_Figure_Brackets_Structure_Definition() {
66       std::cout << remove_leading_numbers(typeid(*this).name()) << " <% ... %>;\n
     ";
67   }
68 %>;
```

This code contains two structures with its constructors. Every constructor prints its class name using typeid **C++** function and our function for removing leading numbers. One of the structures is declared by using primary figure braces and another with alternative figure braces. For classes by default, all members are private but for structures by default they are public → this is the main difference between class and structure in **C++** programming language.

Listing 173. main.cpp#70

```
70 int main() {
```

Declaration of entry point for our **C++** program → function main which returns an integer value and in this case it declared without arguments. From here starting execution of our program. The function main can receive some input parameters like number of command line arguments and an array with the arguments itself.

Like:

```
int main(int arguments_count, char* arguments[]) { ... return 0; }
```

or

```
int main(int arguments_count, char** arguments) { ... return 0; }
```

Listing 174. main.cpp#71..73

```
71    primary_function_definition();
72    alternative_function_definition();
73    std::cout << "\n";
```

Here we call two functions first defined with primary figure braces and second one with alternative braces. The last line prints on the output console an empty new line.

Listing 175. main.cpp#75..83

```
75    const Primary_Figure_Brackets_Class_Definition
76        primary_figure_brackets_class_definition;
77    const Alternative_Figure_Brackets_Class_Definition
78        alternative_figure_brackets_class_definition;
79    Primary_Figure_Brackets_Structure_Definition
80        primary_figure_brackets_structure_definition;
81    Alternative_Figure_Brackets_Structure_Definition
82        alternative_figure_brackets_structure_definition;
83    std::cout << "\n";
```

Here we declare two class constants and two structure variables that activate its constructors and they print its class and structure names. After that, we print the empty new line on the program console. ---

Listing 176. `main.cpp#85..116`

```
85   int number = 10;
86
87   std::cout << "Primary figure brackets '{ " << number << " }'\n";
88
89   <%
90     int number = 20;
91
92     std::cout << "Alternative figure brackets ";
93     std::cout << "'<% ";
94     std::cout << number;
95     std::cout << " %>'\n";
96   %>
97
98   {
99     int number = 30;
100
101    std::cout << "Primary open, alternative close figure brackets ";
102    std::cout << "'{ ";
103    std::cout << number;
104    std::cout << " %>'\n";
105  %>
106
107  <%
108    int number = 40;
109
110    std::cout << "Alternative open, primary close figure brackets ";
111    std::cout << "'<% ";
112    std::cout << number;
113    std::cout << " }'\n";
114  }
115
116  std::cout << "Primary figure brackets '{ " << number << " }'\n\n";
```

Here we print declared variables in different programming blocks with primary and alternative figure brackets. As we can see the values of variables are not visible outside its declaration block.

Listing 177. `main.cpp#118..132`

```
118  // constant initialization:
119  const int primary_initialized_integer_constant{1};
120  std::cout << "primary_initialized_integer_constant{ "
121          << primary_initialized_integer_constant << " }\n";
122  const int alternative_initialized_integer_constant<% 2 %>;
123  std::cout << "alternative_initialized_integer_constant<% "
124          << alternative_initialized_integer_constant << " %>\n\n";
125
126  // variable initialization:
127  int primary_initialized_integer_variable{3};
128  std::cout << "primary_initialized_integer_variable{ "
129          << primary_initialized_integer_variable << " }\n";
130  int alternative_initialized_integer_variable<% 4 %>;
131  std::cout << "alternative_initialized_integer_variable<% "
132          << alternative_initialized_integer_variable << " %>" << std::endl;
```

In this code, we use the primary and alternative figure brackets for the initialization of constants and variables.

Listing 178. `main.cpp#134`

```
134  return EXIT_SUCCESS;
```

In this row, the `main` function returns 0 which normally means that its execution is successful.

Listing 179. `main.cpp#135`

```
135  }
```

This primary closing figure bracket ends the body of `main` function. Here all declared non dynamically allocated variables inside the function body are destructed and all dynamically allocated variables must be destructed too.

4.3. sharp_01 / main.cpp

Listing 180. ~/c++/sources/chapter_02_03_00/sharp_01/main.cpp

```
1  #include <iostream>
2
3  // primary sharp
4  #define TEXT_PRIMARY(item) #item
5
6  // alternative sharp
7  %:define TEXT_ALTERNATIVE(item) %:item
8
9  int main() {
10     int integer_value = 10;
11
12     std::cout << "'#'  " << TEXT_PRIMARY(integer_value) << " = " << integer_value
13             << "\n";
14     std::cout << "'%:' " << TEXT_ALTERNATIVE(integer_value) << " = "
15             << integer_value << "\n\n";
16
17  #ifdef _WIN32
18     std::cout << "Hello from Windows!" << std::endl;
19  %:else
20     std::cout << "Hello from alternative sharp!" << std::endl;
21  %:endif
22
23     return EXIT_SUCCESS;
24  }
```

Example code using basic # and alternative %: operator cas.

Listing 181. main.cpp#1

```
1  #include <iostream>
```

The `include` preprocessing loads **C++** definitions for Input/Output (I/O) operations with streams.

In our program we use only:

- `std::cout` → output stream,
- `<<` → send right operand to the output stream (left operand) and
- `std::endl` → send `new line` to the output stream and flushes stream content.

Listing 182. `main.cpp#3`

```
3 // primary sharp
```

A comment at the end of the line indicates that on the next line, we use the primary sharp operator #.

Listing 183. `main.cpp#4`

```
4 #define TEXT_PRIMARY(item) #item
```

This line sets a preprocessor definition that returns the text passed as its parameter - this way we can get the name of a variable.

Listing 184. `main.cpp#6`

```
6 // alternative sharp
```

A comment at the end of the line indicates that on the next line, we use an alternative to the sharp operator.

Listing 185. `main.cpp#7`

```
/ %:define TEXT_ALTERNATIVE(item) %:item
```

We use an alternative to a hash operator to create a preprocessor directive and return its parameter as text.

Listing 186. `main.cpp#9`

```
9 int main() {
```

Declaration of entry point for our **C++** program → function `main` which returns an integer value and in this case it declared without arguments. From here starting execution of our program. The function `main` can receive some input parameters like number of command line arguments and an array with the arguments itself.

Like:

```
int main(int arguments_count, char* arguments[]) { ... return 0; }
```

or

```
int main(int arguments_count, char** arguments) { ... return 0; }
```

Listing 187. main.cpp#10

```
10   int integer_value = 10;
```

Defines an integer variable to which we assign the value 10.

Listing 188. main.cpp#12..15

```
12   std::cout << "'#'   " << TEXT_PRIMARY(integer_value) << " = " << integer_value
13           << "\n";
14   std::cout << "'%:' " << TEXT_ALTERNATIVE(integer_value) << " = "
15           << integer_value << "\n\n";
```

We output the variable name using the two preprocessor definitions set earlier in the program, then print the equal sign followed by its value.

Listing 189. main.cpp#17..21

```
17  #ifdef _WIN32
18    std::cout << "Hello from Windows!" << std::endl;
19  %:else
20    std::cout << "Hello from alternative sharp!" << std::endl;
21  %:endif
```

We output a greeting message to the console using the primary and an alternative sharp operator.

Listing 190. main.cpp#23

```
23    return EXIT_SUCCESS;
```

Returns successful execution of the program in this case the number 0, which corresponds to the preprocessor definition EXIT_SUCCESS.

Listing 191. main.cpp#24

```
24 }
```

End of main function body.

4.4. double_sharp_01 / main.cpp

Listing 192. ~/c++/sources/chapter_02_04_00/double_sharp_01/main.cpp

```cpp
1 #include <iostream>
2
3 #define STICK_PRIMARY(item_left_part, item_right_part) \
4   item_left_part##item_right_part
5 #define STICK_ALTERNATIVE(item_left_part, item_right_part) \
6   item_left_part%:%:item_right_part
7
8 int main() {
9   std::string hello_world_message = "Hello, World!";
10
11   std::cout << "##   " << STICK_PRIMARY(hello_world, _message) << "\n";
12   std::cout << "%:%: " << STICK_ALTERNATIVE(hello_world, _message) << std::endl;
13
14   return 0;
15 }
```

The above code shows an example of using the basic ## and the alternative %:%: preprocessor concatenation operator - double sharp.

Listing 193. main.cpp#1

```cpp
1 #include <iostream>
```

The include preprocessing loads **C++** definitions for Input/Output (I/O) operations with streams.

In our program we use only:

- std::cout → output stream,

- `<<` → send right operand to the output stream (left operand) and

- `std::endl` → send new line to the output stream and flushes stream content.

Listing 194. main.cpp#3..4

```
3 #define STICK_PRIMARY(item_left_part, item_right_part) \
4   item_left_part##item_right_part
```

Sets a preprocessor definition that concatenates its two arguments into one using the basic concatenation operator `##`. In other words, we can assign a variable name to assemble from several components - in this case, two: a left and a right part.

Listing 195. main.cpp#5..6

```
5 #define STICK_ALTERNATIVE(item_left_part, item_right_part) \
6   item_left_part%:%:item_right_part
```

Specifies a preprocessor definition that concatenates its two arguments into one using the alternative concatenation operator `%:%:`. In other words, we can assign a variable name to assemble from several components - in this case, two: a left and a right part.

Listing 196. main.cpp#8

```
8 int main() {
```

Declaration of entry point for our **C++** program → function main which returns an integer value and in this case it declared without arguments. From here starting execution of our program. The function main can receive some input parameters like number of command line arguments and an array with the arguments itself.

Like:

```
int main(int arguments_count, char* arguments[]) { ... return 0; }
```

or

```
int main(int arguments_count, char** arguments) { ... return 0; }
```

Listing 197. main.cpp#9

```
9    std::string hello_world_message = "Hello, World!";
```

We define a string variable named hello_world_message to which we assign the value Hello, World!.

Listing 198. `main.cpp#11`

```
11   std::cout << "##   " << STICK_PRIMARY(hello_world, _message) << "\n";
```

The `STICK_PRIMARY'` preprocessor directive concatenates the two parts of the variable name and outputs its value.

Listing 199. `main.cpp#12`

```
12   std::cout << "%:%: " << STICK_ALTERNATIVE(hello_world, _message) << std::endl;
```

The `STICK_ALTERNATIVE'` preprocessor directive concatenates the two parts of the variable name and outputs its value as a result.

Listing 200. `main.cpp#14`

```
14   return 0;
```

The execution of the function ends with a result of 0, which means that the program completed successfully.

Listing 201. `main.cpp#15`

```
15 }
```

End of `main` function body.

4.5. logically_and_01 / main.cpp

Listing 202. ~/c++/sources/chapter_02_05_00/logically_and_01/main.cpp

```cpp
#include <bitset>
#include <ciso646>
#include <iomanip>
#include <iostream>
#include <sstream>

const std::string LEFT                      = "left";
const std::string RIGHT                     = "right";
const std::string LEFT_PRIMARY_AND_RIGHT     = LEFT + " && " + RIGHT;
const std::string LEFT_ALTERNATIVE_AND_RIGHT = LEFT + " and " + RIGHT;

template <typename Operand_Type>
auto print(std::string const& operand_name, Operand_Type operand) {
    std::stringstream result;

    result << std::setw(LEFT_ALTERNATIVE_AND_RIGHT.length()) << operand_name
           << " = " << std::dec << std::setw(sizeof(operand) * 3) << +operand;
    result << ", 0x" << std::setfill('0') << std::setw(sizeof(operand) * 2)
           << std::uppercase << std::hex << +operand;
    result << ", 0b" << std::bitset<sizeof(operand) * 8>(operand) << "\n";

    return result;
}

typedef char Integer;

int main() {
    Integer left;
    Integer right;
    long long input;

    std::cout << "Please enter a \"" << LEFT << "\" operand:\n";
    std::cin >> input;
    left = static_cast<Integer>(input);
    std::cout << "and a \"" << RIGHT << "\" operand:\n";
    std::cin >> input;
    right = static_cast<Integer>(input);

    std::cout << std::endl;
    std::cout << print(LEFT, left).rdbuf();
    std::cout << print(RIGHT, right).rdbuf();
```

```
42    std::cout << print(LEFT_PRIMARY_AND_RIGHT,
43                    static_cast<Integer>(left && right))
44                .rdbuf();
45    std::cout << print(LEFT_ALTERNATIVE_AND_RIGHT,
46                    static_cast<Integer>(left and right))
47                .rdbuf();
48
49    return EXIT_SUCCESS;
50 }
```

The above program demonstrates the use of the basic `&&` and the alternative `and` operator for logical AND.

Listing 203. `main.cpp#1`

```
1 #include <bitset>
```

The `include` preprocessing loads **C++** definitions for bit manipulations in our case we use the `std::bitset` to output an integer to the binary format.

Listing 204. `main.cpp#2`

```
2 #include <ciso646>
```

The `include` preprocessing loads **C++** definitions for compatibility header, in C defines alternative operator representations which are keywords in **C++**.
This header was originally in the C standard library as `<iso646.h>`.

<ciso646> is removed in **C++20**.
Corresponding <iso646.h> is still available in **C++20**.

Listing 205. main.cpp#3

```
3 #include <iomanip>
```

The include preprocessing loads **C++** definitions for Input/Output (I/O) manipulators regarding formatiting of the stream I/O operations. We use manipulators like these:

- std::dec - next output is an decimal integer number;
- std::setw - set the width on a next output;
- std::setfill - set the fill character regarding difference between full width from the std::setw and real width of a printed value;
- std::uppercase - set the next output to be uppercase;
- std::hex - next output is an hexa decimal integer number.

Listing 206. main.cpp#4

```
4 #include <iostream>
```

The `include` preprocessing loads **C++** definitions for Input/Output (I/O) operations with streams.

In our program we use only:

- `std::cout` → output stream,
- `<<` → send right operand to the output stream (left operand) and
- `std::endl` → send `new line` to the output stream and flushes stream content.

Listing 207. `main.cpp#5`

```
5 #include <sstream>
```

The 'include' preprocessing command loads the definitions regarding string stream input and output operations.

Listing 208. `main.cpp#7..10`

```
 7 const std::string LEFT                  = "left";
 8 const std::string RIGHT                 = "right";
 9 const std::string LEFT_PRIMARY_AND_RIGHT     = LEFT + " && " + RIGHT;
10 const std::string LEFT_ALTERNATIVE_AND_RIGHT = LEFT + " and " + RIGHT;
```

The string constants declarations.

Listing 209. main.cpp#12..23

```
12 template <typename Operand_Type>
13 auto print(std::string const& operand_name, Operand_Type operand) {
14   std::stringstream result;
15
16   result << std::setw(LEFT_ALTERNATIVE_AND_RIGHT.length()) << operand_name
17        << " = " << std::dec << std::setw(sizeof(operand) * 3) << +operand;
18   result << ", 0x" << std::setfill('0') << std::setw(sizeof(operand) * 2)
19        << std::uppercase << std::hex << +operand;
20   result << ", 0b" << std::bitset<sizeof(operand) * 8>(operand) << "\n";
21
22   return result;
23 }
```

Printing result of an operation.

Listing 210. main.cpp#25

```
25 typedef char Integer;
```

Integer warpper type definition - it can be used for covering different integer **C**++ types.

Listing 211. main.cpp#27..50

```
27 int main() {
28   Integer left;
29   Integer right;
30   long long input;
31
32   std::cout << "Please enter a \"" << LEFT << "\" operand:\n";
33   std::cin >> input;
34   left = static_cast<Integer>(input);
35   std::cout << "and a \"" << RIGHT << "\" operand:\n";
36   std::cin >> input;
37   right = static_cast<Integer>(input);
38
39   std::cout << std::endl;
40   std::cout << print(LEFT, left).rdbuf();
41   std::cout << print(RIGHT, right).rdbuf();
```

```
42   std::cout << print(LEFT_PRIMARY_AND_RIGHT,
43                       static_cast<Integer>(left && right))
44                  .rdbuf();
45   std::cout << print(LEFT_ALTERNATIVE_AND_RIGHT,
46                       static_cast<Integer>(left and right))
47                  .rdbuf();
48
49   return EXIT_SUCCESS;
50 }
```

This is the `main` function, which is the entry point into program execution. In it, the program simply reads two integers and performs the operation logically and by using the basic and alternative `and' operators, outputting the result of both equivalent operations, and the result must be the same.

4.6. bitwise_and_01 / main.cpp

Listing 212. ~/c++/sources/chapter_02_06_00/bitwise_and_01/main.cpp

```cpp
#include <bitset>
#include <ciso646>
#include <iomanip>
#include <iostream>
#include <sstream>

const std::string LEFT                                = "left";
const std::string RIGHT                               = "right";
const std::string LEFT_PRIMARY_BITWISE_AND_RIGHT      = LEFT + " & " + RIGHT;
const std::string LEFT_ALTERNATIVE_BITWISE_AND_RIGHT = LEFT + " bitand " +
  RIGHT;

template <typename Operand_Type>
auto print(std::string const& operand_name, Operand_Type operand) {
  std::stringstream result;

  result << std::setw(LEFT_ALTERNATIVE_BITWISE_AND_RIGHT.length())
         << operand_name << " = " << std::dec << std::setw(sizeof(operand) * 3)
         << +operand;
  result << ", 0x" << std::setfill('0') << std::setw(sizeof(operand) * 2)
         << std::uppercase << std::hex << +operand;
  result << ", 0b" << std::bitset<sizeof(operand) * 8>(operand) << "\n";

  return result;
}

typedef char Integer;

int main() {
  Integer left;
  Integer right;
  long long input;

  std::cout << "Please enter a \"" << LEFT << "\" operand:\n";
  std::cin >> input;
  left = static_cast<Integer>(input);
  std::cout << "and a \"" << RIGHT << "\" operand:\n";
  std::cin >> input;
  right = static_cast<Integer>(input);

  std::cout << std::endl;
```

```
41  std::cout << print(LEFT, left).rdbuf();
42  std::cout << print(RIGHT, right).rdbuf();
43  std::cout << print(LEFT_PRIMARY_BITWISE_AND_RIGHT,
44                  static_cast<Integer>(left & right))
45              .rdbuf();
46  std::cout << print(LEFT_ALTERNATIVE_BITWISE_AND_RIGHT,
47                  static_cast<Integer>(left bitand right))
48              .rdbuf();
49
50  return EXIT_SUCCESS;
51 }
```

The above program demonstrates the use of the basic and alternate operators for bitwise and.

Listing 213. `main.cpp#1`

```
1 #include <bitset>
```

The `include` preprocessing loads **C++** definitions for bit manipulations in our case we use the `std::bitset` to output an integer to the binary format.

Listing 214. `main.cpp#2`

```
2 #include <ciso646>
```

The `include` preprocessing loads **C++** definitions for compatibility header, in C defines alternative operator representations which are keywords in **C++**.
This header was originally in the C standard library as `<iso646.h>`.

`<ciso646>` is removed in **C++20**.
Corresponding `<iso646.h>` is still available in **C++20**.

Listing 215. main.cpp#3

```
3 #include <iomanip>
```

The `include` preprocessing loads **C++** definitions for Input/Output (I/O) manipulators regarding formatiting of the stream I/O operations. We use manipulators like these:

- `std::dec` - next output is an decimal integer number;
- `std::setw` - set the width on a next output;
- `std::setfill` - set the fill character regarding difference between full width from the `std::setw` and real width of a printed value;
- `std::uppercase` - set the next output to be uppercase;
- `std::hex` - next output is an hexa decimal integer number.

Listing 216. main.cpp#4

```
4 #include <iostream>
```

The include preprocessing loads **C++** definitions for Input/Output (I/O) operations with streams.

In our program we use only:

- std::cout → output stream,
- << → send right operand to the output stream (left operand) and
- std::endl → send new line to the output stream and flushes stream content.

Listing 217. main.cpp#5

```
5 #include <sstream>
```

The 'include' preprocessing command loads the definitions regarding string stream input and output operations.

Listing 218. main.cpp#7..11

```
 7 const std::string LEFT                            = "left";
 8 const std::string RIGHT                           = "right";
 9 const std::string LEFT_PRIMARY_BITWISE_AND_RIGHT   = LEFT + " & " + RIGHT;
10 const std::string LEFT_ALTERNATIVE_BITWISE_AND_RIGHT = LEFT + " bitand " +
   RIGHT;
```

The string constants declarations.

Listing 219. `main.cpp#13..25`

```cpp
13 auto print(std::string const& operand_name, Operand_Type operand) {
14    std::stringstream result;
15
16    result << std::setw(LEFT_ALTERNATIVE_BITWISE_AND_RIGHT.length())
17           << operand_name << " = " << std::dec << std::setw(sizeof(operand) * 3)
18           << +operand;
19    result << ", 0x" << std::setfill('0') << std::setw(sizeof(operand) * 2)
20           << std::uppercase << std::hex << +operand;
21    result << ", 0b" << std::bitset<sizeof(operand) * 8>(operand) << "\n";
22
23    return result;
24 }
```

Printing result of an operation.

Listing 220. `main.cpp#27`

Integer warpper type definition - it can be used
for covering different integer **C**++ types.

Listing 221. `main.cpp#29..52`

```cpp
29    Integer left;
30    Integer right;
31    long long input;
32
33    std::cout << "Please enter a \"" << LEFT << "\" operand:\n";
34    std::cin >> input;
35    left = static_cast<Integer>(input);
36    std::cout << "and a \"" << RIGHT << "\" operand:\n";
37    std::cin >> input;
38    right = static_cast<Integer>(input);
39
40    std::cout << std::endl;
41    std::cout << print(LEFT, left).rdbuf();
42    std::cout << print(RIGHT, right).rdbuf();
43    std::cout << print(LEFT_PRIMARY_BITWISE_AND_RIGHT,
44                       static_cast<Integer>(left & right))
```

```
45                      .rdbuf();
46   std::cout << print(LEFT_ALTERNATIVE_BITWISE_AND_RIGHT,
47                      static_cast<Integer>(left bitand right))
48                      .rdbuf();
49
50   return EXIT_SUCCESS;
51 }
```

This is the main function, which is the entry point into program execution. In it, the program simply reads two integers and performs the operation bitwise and by using the basic and alternate bitwise operators and outputting the result of both equivalent operations, the result must be the same.

4.7.
bitwise_and_with_acquisit ion_01 / main.cpp

Listing 222.

~/c++/sources/chapter_02_07_00/bitwise_and_with_acquisition_01/main.cpp

```cpp
 1  #include <bitset>
 2  #include <ciso646>
 3  #include <iomanip>
 4  #include <iostream>
 5  #include <sstream>
 6
 7  const std::string LEFT                            = "left";
 8  const std::string RIGHT                           = "right";
 9  const std::string LEFT_PRIMARY_BITWISE_AND_RIGHT     = LEFT + " &= " + RIGHT;
10  const std::string LEFT_ALTERNATIVE_BITWISE_AND_RIGHT = LEFT + " and_eq " +
    RIGHT;
11
12  template <typename Operand_Type>
13  auto print(std::string const& operand_name, Operand_Type operand) {
14      std::stringstream result;
15
16      result << std::setw(LEFT_ALTERNATIVE_BITWISE_AND_RIGHT.length())
17              << operand_name << " = " << std::dec << std::setw(sizeof(operand) * 3)
18              << +operand;
19      result << ", 0x" << std::setfill('0') << std::setw(sizeof(operand) * 2)
20              << std::uppercase << std::hex << +operand;
21      result << ", 0b" << std::bitset<sizeof(operand) * 8>(operand) << "\n";
22
23      return result;
24  }
25
26  typedef char Integer;
27
28  int main() {
29      Integer left;
30      Integer right;
31      long long input;
32
33      std::cout << "Please enter a \"" << LEFT << "\" operand:\n";
34      std::cin >> input;
35      left = static_cast<Integer>(input);
36      std::cout << "and a \"" << RIGHT << "\" operand:\n";
```

```
37    std::cin >> input;
38    right = static_cast<Integer>(input);
39
40    std::cout << std::endl;
41    std::cout << print(LEFT, left).rdbuf();
42    std::cout << print(RIGHT, right).rdbuf();
43
44    Integer result = left;
45    result &= right;
46    std::cout << print(LEFT_PRIMARY_BITWISE_AND_RIGHT, result).rdbuf();
47
48    result = left;
49    result and_eq right;
50    std::cout << print(LEFT_ALTERNATIVE_BITWISE_AND_RIGHT, result).rdbuf();
51
52    return EXIT_SUCCESS;
53 }
```

The above example program shows the use of the bitwise operator with assignment as well.

Listing 223. main.cpp#1

```
1 #include <bitset>
```

The include preprocessing loads **C++** definitions for bit manipulations in our case we use the std::bitset to output an integer to the binary format.

Listing 224. main.cpp#2

```
2 #include <ciso646>
```

The include preprocessing loads **C++** definitions for compatibility header, in C defines alternative operator representations which are keywords in **C++**.

This header was originally in the C standard library as `<iso646.h>`.

`<ciso646>` is removed in **C++20**.

Corresponding `<iso646.h>` is still available in **C++20**.

Listing 225. `main.cpp#3`

```
3 #include <iomanip>
```

The `include` preprocessing loads **C++** definitions for Input/Output (I/O) manipulators regarding formatiting of the stream I/O operations. We use manipulators like these:

- `std::dec` - next output is an decimal integer number;

- `std::setw` - set the width on a next output;

- `std::setfill` - set the fill character regarding difference between full width from the `std::setw` and real width of a printed value;

- `std::uppercase` - set the next output to be uppercase;

- `std::hex` - next output is an hexa decimal integer number.

Listing 226. `main.cpp#4`

```
4 #include <iostream>
```

The `include` preprocessing loads **C**++ definitions for Input/Output (I/O) operations with streams.

In our program we use only:

- `std::cout` → output stream,
- `<<` → send right operand to the output stream (left operand) and
- `std::endl` → send `new line` to the output stream and flushes stream content.

Listing 227. `main.cpp#5`

```
5 #include <sstream>
```

The 'include' preprocessing command loads the definitions regarding string stream input and output operations.

Listing 228. `main.cpp#7..11`

```
 7 const std::string LEFT                             = "left";
 8 const std::string RIGHT                            = "right";
 9 const std::string LEFT_PRIMARY_BITWISE_AND_RIGHT    = LEFT + " &= " + RIGHT;
10 const std::string LEFT_ALTERNATIVE_BITWISE_AND_RIGHT = LEFT + " and_eq " +
   RIGHT;
```

The string constants declarations.

Listing 229. main.cpp#13..25

```
13  auto print(std::string const& operand_name, Operand_Type operand) {
14    std::stringstream result;
15
16    result << std::setw(LEFT_ALTERNATIVE_BITWISE_AND_RIGHT.length())
17          << operand_name << " = " << std::dec << std::setw(sizeof(operand) * 3)
18          << +operand;
19    result << ", 0x" << std::setfill('0') << std::setw(sizeof(operand) * 2)
20          << std::uppercase << std::hex << +operand;
21    result << ", 0b" << std::bitset<sizeof(operand) * 8>(operand) << "\n";
22
23    return result;
24  }
```

Printing result of an operation.

Listing 230. main.cpp#27

Integer warpper type definition - it can be used for covering different integer C++ types.

Listing 231. main.cpp#29..54

```
29    Integer left;
30    Integer right;
31    long long input;
32
33    std::cout << "Please enter a \"" << LEFT << "\" operand:\n";
34    std::cin >> input;
35    left = static_cast<Integer>(input);
36    std::cout << "and a \"" << RIGHT << "\" operand:\n";
37    std::cin >> input;
38    right = static_cast<Integer>(input);
39
40    std::cout << std::endl;
41    std::cout << print(LEFT, left).rdbuf();
```

```
42   std::cout << print(RIGHT, right).rdbuf();
43
44   Integer result = left;
45   result &= right;
46   std::cout << print(LEFT_PRIMARY_BITWISE_AND_RIGHT, result).rdbuf();
47
48   result = left;
49   result and_eq right;
50   std::cout << print(LEFT_ALTERNATIVE_BITWISE_AND_RIGHT, result).rdbuf();
51
52   return EXIT_SUCCESS;
53 }
```

This is the `main` function, which is the entry point into program execution. In it, the program simply reads two integers and performs the bitwise and assignment operation, using the basic and alternate bitwise operators and taking the result of both equivalent operations, and the result should be the same.

...

4.8. logically_or_01 / main.cpp

Listing 232. ~/c++/sources/chapter_02_08_00/logically_or_01/main.cpp

```cpp
1  #include <bitset>
2  #include <ciso646>
3  #include <iomanip>
4  #include <iostream>
5  #include <sstream>
6
7  const std::string LEFT                    = "left";
8  const std::string RIGHT                   = "right";
9  const std::string LEFT_PRIMARY_OR_RIGHT   = LEFT + " || " + RIGHT;
10 const std::string LEFT_ALTERNATIVE_OR_RIGHT = LEFT + " or " + RIGHT;
11
12 template <typename Operand_Type>
13 auto print(std::string const& operand_name, Operand_Type operand) {
14   std::stringstream result;
15
16   result << std::setw(LEFT_ALTERNATIVE_OR_RIGHT.length()) << operand_name
17          << " = " << std::dec << std::setw(sizeof(operand) * 3) << +operand;
18   result << ", 0x" << std::setfill('0') << std::setw(sizeof(operand) * 2)
19          << std::uppercase << std::hex << +operand;
20   result << ", 0b" << std::bitset<sizeof(operand) * 8>(operand) << "\n";
21
22   return result;
23 }
24
25 typedef char Integer;
26
27 int main() {
28   Integer left;
29   Integer right;
30   long long input;
31
32   std::cout << "Please enter a \"" << LEFT << "\" operand:\n";
33   std::cin >> input;
34   left = static_cast<Integer>(input);
35   std::cout << "and a \"" << RIGHT << "\" operand:\n";
36   std::cin >> input;
37   right = static_cast<Integer>(input);
38
39   std::cout << std::endl;
40   std::cout << print(LEFT, left).rdbuf();
41   std::cout << print(RIGHT, right).rdbuf();
```

```
42   std::cout << print(LEFT_PRIMARY_OR_RIGHT, static_cast<Integer>(left || right))
43               .rdbuf();
44   std::cout << print(LEFT_ALTERNATIVE_OR_RIGHT,
45                   static_cast<Integer>(left or right))
46               .rdbuf();
47
48   return EXIT_SUCCESS;
49 }
```

The above program demonstrates the use of the basic || and the alternative or operator for logical or.

Listing 233. main.cpp#1

```
1 #include <bitset>
```

The include preprocessing loads **C++** definitions for bit manipulations in our case we use the std::bitset to output an integer to the binary format.

Listing 234. main.cpp#2

```
2 #include <ciso646>
```

The include preprocessing loads **C++** definitions for compatibility header, in C defines alternative operator representations which are keywords in **C++**.
This header was originally in the C standard library as <iso646.h>.

`<ciso646>` is removed in **C++20**.
Corresponding `<iso646.h>` is still available in **C++20**.

Listing 235. main.cpp#3

```
3 #include <iomanip>
```

The `include` preprocessing loads **C++** definitions for Input/Output (I/O) manipulators regarding formatiting of the stream I/O operations. We use manipulators like these:

- `std::dec` - next output is an decimal integer number;
- `std::setw` - set the width on a next output;
- `std::setfill` - set the fill character regarding difference between full width from the `std::setw` and real width of a printed value;
- `std::uppercase` - set the next output to be uppercase;
- `std::hex` - next output is an hexa decimal integer number.

Listing 236. main.cpp#4

```
4 #include <iostream>
```

The `include` preprocessing loads **C++** definitions for Input/Output (I/O) operations with streams.

In our program we use only:

- `std::cout` → output stream,
- `<<` → send right operand to the output stream (left operand) and
- `std::endl` → send `new line` to the output stream and flushes stream content.

Listing 237. `main.cpp#5`

```
5 #include <sstream>
```

The 'include' preprocessing command loads the definitions regarding string stream input and output operations.

Listing 238. `main.cpp#7..10`

```
7  const std::string LEFT                   = "left";
8  const std::string RIGHT                  = "right";
9  const std::string LEFT_PRIMARY_OR_RIGHT     = LEFT + " || " + RIGHT;
10 const std::string LEFT_ALTERNATIVE_OR_RIGHT = LEFT + " or " + RIGHT;
```

The string constants declarations.

Listing 239. `main.cpp#12..23`

```cpp
12 template <typename Operand_Type>
13 auto print(std::string const& operand_name, Operand_Type operand) {
14     std::stringstream result;
15
16     result << std::setw(LEFT_ALTERNATIVE_OR_RIGHT.length()) << operand_name
17            << " = " << std::dec << std::setw(sizeof(operand) * 3) << +operand;
18     result << ", 0x" << std::setfill('0') << std::setw(sizeof(operand) * 2)
19            << std::uppercase << std::hex << +operand;
20     result << ", 0b" << std::bitset<sizeof(operand) * 8>(operand) << "\n";
21
22     return result;
23 }
```

Printing result of an operation.

Listing 240. `main.cpp#25`

```cpp
25 typedef char Integer;
```

Integer warpper type definition - it can be used for covering different integer C++ types.

Listing 241. `main.cpp#27..49`

```cpp
27 int main() {
28     Integer left;
29     Integer right;
30     long long input;
31
32     std::cout << "Please enter a \"" << LEFT << "\" operand:\n";
33     std::cin >> input;
34     left = static_cast<Integer>(input);
35     std::cout << "and a \"" << RIGHT << "\" operand:\n";
36     std::cin >> input;
37     right = static_cast<Integer>(input);
38
39     std::cout << std::endl;
40     std::cout << print(LEFT, left).rdbuf();
41     std::cout << print(RIGHT, right).rdbuf();
```

```
42    std::cout << print(LEFT_PRIMARY_OR_RIGHT, static_cast<Integer>(left || right))
43                    .rdbuf();
44    std::cout << print(LEFT_ALTERNATIVE_OR_RIGHT,
45                    static_cast<Integer>(left or right))
46                    .rdbuf();
47
48    return EXIT_SUCCESS;
49 }
```

This is the `main` function, which is the entry point into program execution. In it, the program simply reads two integers and performs the logical or operation, using the basic and alternate bitwise or operators, and returns the result of the two equivalent operations, the result of which must be the same.

...

4.9. bitwise_or_01 / main.cpp

Listing 242. ~/c++/sources/chapter_02_09_00/bitwise_or_01/main.cpp

```cpp
#include <bitset>
#include <ciso646>
#include <iomanip>
#include <iostream>
#include <sstream>

const std::string LEFT                          = "left";
const std::string RIGHT                         = "right";
const std::string LEFT_PRIMARY_BITWISE_OR_RIGHT     = LEFT + " | " + RIGHT;
const std::string LEFT_ALTERNATIVE_BITWISE_OR_RIGHT = LEFT + " bitor " + RIGHT;

template <typename Operand_Type>
auto print(std::string const& operand_name, Operand_Type operand) {
  std::stringstream result;

  result << std::setw(LEFT_ALTERNATIVE_BITWISE_OR_RIGHT.length())
         << operand_name << " = " << std::dec << std::setw(sizeof(operand) * 3)
         << +operand;
  result << ", 0x" << std::setfill('0') << std::setw(sizeof(operand) * 2)
         << std::uppercase << std::hex << +operand;
  result << ", 0b" << std::bitset<sizeof(operand) * 8>(operand) << "\n";

  return result;
}

typedef char Integer;

int main() {
  Integer left;
  Integer right;
  long long input;

  std::cout << "Please enter a \"" << LEFT << "\" operand:\n";
  std::cin >> input;
  left = static_cast<Integer>(input);
  std::cout << "and a \"" << RIGHT << "\" operand:\n";
  std::cin >> input;
  right = static_cast<Integer>(input);

  std::cout << std::endl;
  std::cout << print(LEFT, left).rdbuf();
```

```
42    std::cout << print(RIGHT, right).rdbuf();
43    std::cout << print(LEFT_PRIMARY_BITWISE_OR_RIGHT,
44                    static_cast<Integer>(left | right))
45                .rdbuf();
46    std::cout << print(LEFT_ALTERNATIVE_BITWISE_OR_RIGHT,
47                    static_cast<Integer>(left bitor right))
48                .rdbuf();
49
50    return EXIT_SUCCESS;
51 }
```

The above example program shows the use of the bitwise operator or.

Listing 243. main.cpp#1

```
1 #include <bitset>
```

The include preprocessing loads **C++** definitions for bit manipulations in our case we use the std::bitset to output an integer to the binary format.

Listing 244. main.cpp#2

```
2 #include <ciso646>
```

The include preprocessing loads **C++** definitions for compatibility header, in C defines alternative operator representations which are keywords in **C++**.
This header was originally in the C standard library as <iso646.h>.

`<ciso646>` is removed in **C++20**.
Corresponding `<iso646.h>` is still available in **C++20**.

Listing 245. main.cpp#3

```
3 #include <iomanip>
```

The `include` preprocessing loads **C++** definitions for Input/Output (I/O) manipulators regarding formatiting of the stream I/O operations. We use manipulators like these:

- `std::dec` - next output is an decimal integer number;
- `std::setw` - set the width on a next output;
- `std::setfill` - set the fill character regarding difference between full width from the `std::setw` and real width of a printed value;
- `std::uppercase` - set the next output to be uppercase;
- `std::hex` - next output is an hexa decimal integer number.

Listing 246. main.cpp#4

```
4 #include <iostream>
```

The `include` preprocessing loads **C++** definitions for Input/Output (I/O) operations with streams.

In our program we use only:

- `std::cout` → output stream,
- `<<` → send right operand to the output stream (left operand) and
- `std::endl` → send `new line` to the output stream and flushes stream content.

Listing 247. `main.cpp#5`

```
5 #include <sstream>
```

The 'include' preprocessing command loads the definitions regarding string stream input and output operations.

Listing 248. `main.cpp#7..10`

```
 7 const std::string LEFT                            = "left";
 8 const std::string RIGHT                           = "right";
 9 const std::string LEFT_PRIMARY_BITWISE_OR_RIGHT   = LEFT + " | " + RIGHT;
10 const std::string LEFT_ALTERNATIVE_BITWISE_OR_RIGHT = LEFT + " bitor " + RIGHT;
```

The string constants declarations.

Listing 249. `main.cpp#12..24`

```cpp
12 template <typename Operand_Type>
13 auto print(std::string const& operand_name, Operand_Type operand) {
14   std::stringstream result;
15
16   result << std::setw(LEFT_ALTERNATIVE_BITWISE_OR_RIGHT.length())
17         << operand_name << " = " << std::dec << std::setw(sizeof(operand) * 3)
18         << +operand;
19   result << ", 0x" << std::setfill('0') << std::setw(sizeof(operand) * 2)
20         << std::uppercase << std::hex << +operand;
21   result << ", 0b" << std::bitset<sizeof(operand) * 8>(operand) << "\n";
22
23   return result;
24 }
```

Printing result of an operation.

Listing 250. `main.cpp#26`

```cpp
26 typedef char Integer;
```

Integer warpper type definition - it can be used for covering different integer **C**++ types.

Listing 251. `main.cpp#28..51`

```cpp
28 int main() {
29   Integer left;
30   Integer right;
31   long long input;
32
33   std::cout << "Please enter a \"" << LEFT << "\" operand:\n";
34   std::cin >> input;
35   left = static_cast<Integer>(input);
36   std::cout << "and a \"" << RIGHT << "\" operand:\n";
37   std::cin >> input;
38   right = static_cast<Integer>(input);
39
40   std::cout << std::endl;
41   std::cout << print(LEFT, left).rdbuf();
```

```
42    std::cout << print(RIGHT, right).rdbuf();
43    std::cout << print(LEFT_PRIMARY_BITWISE_OR_RIGHT,
44                    static_cast<Integer>(left | right))
45                    .rdbuf();
46    std::cout << print(LEFT_ALTERNATIVE_BITWISE_OR_RIGHT,
47                    static_cast<Integer>(left bitor right))
48                    .rdbuf();
49
50    return EXIT_SUCCESS;
51  }
```

This is the `main` function, which is the entry point into program execution. In it, the program simply reads two integers and performs the bitwise operation, or, by using the basic and alternate bitwise operators, or by taking the result of both equivalent operations, the result should be the same.

...

4.10.
bitwise_or_with_acquisitio n_01 / main.cpp

Listing 252.

~/c++/sources/chapter_02_10_00/bitwise_or_with_acquisition_01/main.cpp

```cpp
#include <bitset>
#include <ciso646>
#include <iomanip>
#include <iostream>
#include <sstream>

const std::string LEFT                          = "left";
const std::string RIGHT                         = "right";
const std::string LEFT_PRIMARY_BITWISE_OR_RIGHT     = LEFT + " |= " + RIGHT;
const std::string LEFT_ALTERNATIVE_BITWISE_OR_RIGHT = LEFT + " or_eq " + RIGHT;

template <typename Operand_Type>
auto print(std::string const& operand_name, Operand_Type operand) {
    std::stringstream result;

    result << std::setw(LEFT_ALTERNATIVE_BITWISE_OR_RIGHT.length())
           << operand_name << " = " << std::dec << std::setw(sizeof(operand) * 3)
           << +operand;
    result << ", 0x" << std::setfill('0') << std::setw(sizeof(operand) * 2)
           << std::uppercase << std::hex << +operand;
    result << ", 0b" << std::bitset<sizeof(operand) * 8>(operand) << "\n";

    return result;
}

typedef char Integer;

int main() {
    Integer left;
    Integer right;
    long long input;

    std::cout << "Please enter a \"" << LEFT << "\" operand:\n";
    std::cin >> input;
    left = static_cast<Integer>(input);
    std::cout << "and a \"" << RIGHT << "\" operand:\n";
    std::cin >> input;
```

```
38   right = static_cast<Integer>(input);
39
40   std::cout << std::endl;
41   std::cout << print(LEFT, left).rdbuf();
42   std::cout << print(RIGHT, right).rdbuf();
43
44   Integer result = left;
45   result |= right;
46   std::cout << print(LEFT_PRIMARY_BITWISE_OR_RIGHT, result).rdbuf();
47
48   result = left;
49   result or_eq right;
50   std::cout << print(LEFT_ALTERNATIVE_BITWISE_OR_RIGHT, result).rdbuf();
51
52   return EXIT_SUCCESS;
53 }
```

The above sample program shows the use of the bitwise or assignment operator.

Listing 253. main.cpp#1

```
1 #include <bitset>
```

The include preprocessing loads **C++** definitions for bit manipulations in our case we use the std::bitset to output an integer to the binary format.

Listing 254. main.cpp#2

```
2 #include <ciso646>
```

The include preprocessing loads **C++** definitions for compatibility header, in C defines alternative operator representations which are keywords in **C++**.

This header was originally in the C standard library as `<iso646.h>`.

`<ciso646>` is removed in **C++20**.

Corresponding `<iso646.h>` is still available in **C++20**.

Listing 255. `main.cpp#3`

```
#include <iomanip>
```

The `include` preprocessing loads **C++** definitions for Input/Output (I/O) manipulators regarding formatiting of the stream I/O operations. We use manipulators like these:

- `std::dec` - next output is an decimal integer number;

- `std::setw` - set the width on a next output;

- `std::setfill` - set the fill character regarding difference between full width from the `std::setw` and real width of a printed value;

- `std::uppercase` - set the next output to be uppercase;

- `std::hex` - next output is an hexa decimal integer number.

Listing 256. main.cpp#4

```
4 #include <iostream>
```

The `include` preprocessing loads **C++** definitions for Input/Output (I/O) operations with streams.

In our program we use only:

- `std::cout` → output stream,
- `<<` → send right operand to the output stream (left operand) and
- `std::endl` → send `new` `line` to the output stream and flushes stream content.

Listing 257. main.cpp#5

```
5 #include <sstream>
```

The 'include' preprocessing command loads the definitions regarding string stream input and output operations.

Listing 258. main.cpp#12..24

```
12 template <typename Operand_Type>
13 auto print(std::string const& operand_name, Operand_Type operand) {
14   std::stringstream result;
15
16   result << std::setw(LEFT_ALTERNATIVE_BITWISE_OR_RIGHT.length())
17          << operand_name << " = " << std::dec << std::setw(sizeof(operand) * 3)
18          << +operand;
19   result << ", 0x" << std::setfill('0') << std::setw(sizeof(operand) * 2)
```

```
20          << std::uppercase << std::hex << +operand;
21   result << ", 0b" << std::bitset<sizeof(operand) * 8>(operand) << "\n";
22
23   return result;
24 }
```

Printing result of an operation.

Listing 259. `main.cpp#26`

```
26 typedef char Integer;
```

Integer warpper type definition - it can be used for covering different integer C++ types.

Listing 260. `main.cpp#28..53`

```
28 int main() {
29   Integer left;
30   Integer right;
31   long long input;
32
33   std::cout << "Please enter a \"" << LEFT << "\" operand:\n";
34   std::cin >> input;
35   left = static_cast<Integer>(input);
36   std::cout << "and a \"" << RIGHT << "\" operand:\n";
37   std::cin >> input;
38   right = static_cast<Integer>(input);
39
40   std::cout << std::endl;
41   std::cout << print(LEFT, left).rdbuf();
42   std::cout << print(RIGHT, right).rdbuf();
43
44   Integer result = left;
45   result |= right;
46   std::cout << print(LEFT_PRIMARY_BITWISE_OR_RIGHT, result).rdbuf();
47
48   result = left;
49   result or_eq right;
50   std::cout << print(LEFT_ALTERNATIVE_BITWISE_OR_RIGHT, result).rdbuf();
51
```

```
52    return EXIT_SUCCESS;
53 }
```

This is the `main` function, which is the entry point into program execution. In it, the program simply reads two integers and performs the bitwise or assignment operation, using the basic and alternate bitwise or assignment operators, taking the result of both equivalent operations, the result should be the same.

4.11.
bitwise_exclusionary_or_0
1 / main.cpp

Listing 261.
~/c++/sources/chapter_02_11_00/bitwise_exclusionary_or_01/main.cpp

```
 1 #include <bitset>
 2 #include <ciso646>
 3 #include <iomanip>
 4 #include <iostream>
 5 #include <sstream>
 6
 7 const std::string LEFT                                        = "left";
 8 const std::string RIGHT                                       = "right";
 9 const std::string LEFT_PRIMARY_BITWISE_EXCLUSIONARY_OR_RIGHT     = LEFT + " ^ "
   + RIGHT;
10 const std::string LEFT_ALTERNATIVE_BITWISE_EXCLUSIONARY_OR_RIGHT = LEFT + " xor
   " + RIGHT;
11
12 template <typename Operand_Type>
13 auto print(std::string const& operand_name, Operand_Type operand) {
14    std::stringstream result;
15
16    result << std::setw(LEFT_ALTERNATIVE_BITWISE_EXCLUSIONARY_OR_RIGHT.length())
17           << operand_name << " = " << std::dec << std::setw(sizeof(operand) * 3)
18           << +operand;
19    result << ", 0x" << std::setfill('0') << std::setw(sizeof(operand) * 2)
20           << std::uppercase << std::hex << +operand;
21    result << ", 0b" << std::bitset<sizeof(operand) * 8>(operand) << "\n";
22
23    return result;
24 }
25
26 typedef char Integer;
27
28 int main() {
29    Integer left;
30    Integer right;
31    long long input;
32
33    std::cout << "Please enter a \"" << LEFT << "\" operand:\n";
34    std::cin >> input;
35    left = static_cast<Integer>(input);
```

```
36    std::cout << "and a \"" << RIGHT << "\" operand:\n";
37    std::cin >> input;
38    right = static_cast<Integer>(input);
39
40    std::cout << std::endl;
41    std::cout << print(LEFT, left).rdbuf();
42    std::cout << print(RIGHT, right).rdbuf();
43    std::cout << print(LEFT_PRIMARY_BITWISE_EXCLUSIONARY_OR_RIGHT,
44                       static_cast<Integer>(left ^ right))
45                  .rdbuf();
46    std::cout << print(LEFT_ALTERNATIVE_BITWISE_EXCLUSIONARY_OR_RIGHT,
47                       static_cast<Integer>(left xor right))
48                  .rdbuf();
49
50    return EXIT_SUCCESS;
51 }
```

The above example program shows the use of the bitwise exclusive or operator.

Listing 262. `main.cpp#1`

```
1 #include <bitset>
```

The `include` preprocessing loads **C++** definitions for bit manipulations in our case we use the `std::bitset` to output an integer to the binary format.

Listing 263. `main.cpp#2`

```
2 #include <ciso646>
```

The `include` preprocessing loads **C++** definitions for compatibility header, in C defines alternative operator representations which are keywords in **C++**.

This header was originally in the C standard library as `<iso646.h>`.

`<ciso646>` is removed in **C++20**.

Corresponding `<iso646.h>` is still available in **C++20**.

Listing 264. `main.cpp#3`

```
3 #include <iomanip>
```

The `include` preprocessing loads **C++** definitions for Input/Output (I/O) manipulators regarding formatiting of the stream I/O operations. We use manipulators like these:

- `std::dec` - next output is an decimal integer number;

- `std::setw` - set the width on a next output;

- `std::setfill` - set the fill character regarding difference between full width from the `std::setw` and real width of a printed value;

- `std::uppercase` - set the next output to be uppercase;

- `std::hex` - next output is an hexa decimal integer number.

Listing 265. `main.cpp#4`

```
4 #include <iostream>
```

The `include` preprocessing loads **C++** definitions for Input/Output (I/O) operations with streams.

In our program we use only:

- `std::cout` → output stream,
- `<<` → send right operand to the output stream (left operand) and
- `std::endl` → **send** `new line` to the output stream and flushes stream content.

Listing 266. `main.cpp#5`

```
5 #include <sstream>
```

The 'include' preprocessing command loads the definitions regarding string stream input and output operations.

Listing 267. `main.cpp#7..12`

```
 7 const std::string LEFT                                       = "left";
 8 const std::string RIGHT                                      = "right";
 9 const std::string LEFT_PRIMARY_BITWISE_EXCLUSIONARY_OR_RIGHT   = LEFT + " ^ "
   + RIGHT;
10 const std::string LEFT_ALTERNATIVE_BITWISE_EXCLUSIONARY_OR_RIGHT = LEFT + " xor
   " + RIGHT;
11
12 template <typename Operand_Type>
```

The string constants declarations.

Listing 268. `main.cpp#14..26`

```
14   std::stringstream result;
15
16   result << std::setw(LEFT_ALTERNATIVE_BITWISE_EXCLUSIONARY_OR_RIGHT.length())
17           << operand_name << " = " << std::dec << std::setw(sizeof(operand) * 3)
18           << +operand;
19   result << ", 0x" << std::setfill('0') << std::setw(sizeof(operand) * 2)
20           << std::uppercase << std::hex << +operand;
21   result << ", 0b" << std::bitset<sizeof(operand) * 8>(operand) << "\n";
22
23   return result;
24 }
25
26 typedef char Integer;
```

Printing result of an operation.

Listing 269. `main.cpp#28`

```
28 int main() {
```

Integer warpper type definition - it can be used for covering different integer **C++** types.

Listing 270. `main.cpp#30..53`

```
30   Integer right;
31   long long input;
32
33   std::cout << "Please enter a \"" << LEFT << "\" operand:\n";
34   std::cin >> input;
35   left = static_cast<Integer>(input);
36   std::cout << "and a \"" << RIGHT << "\" operand:\n";
37   std::cin >> input;
```

```
38   right = static_cast<Integer>(input);
39
40   std::cout << std::endl;
41   std::cout << print(LEFT, left).rdbuf();
42   std::cout << print(RIGHT, right).rdbuf();
43   std::cout << print(LEFT_PRIMARY_BITWISE_EXCLUSIONARY_OR_RIGHT,
44                      static_cast<Integer>(left ^ right))
45                 .rdbuf();
46   std::cout << print(LEFT_ALTERNATIVE_BITWISE_EXCLUSIONARY_OR_RIGHT,
47                      static_cast<Integer>(left xor right))
48                 .rdbuf();
49
50   return EXIT_SUCCESS;
51 }
```

This is the `main` function, which is the entry point into program execution. In it, the program simply reads two integers and performs the bitwise exclusion operation, or, using the basic and alternate bitwise exclusion operators, outputs the result of both equivalent operations, the result must be the same.

4.12. bitwise_exclusionary_or_ with_acquisition_01 / main.cpp

Listing 271.

~/c++/sources/chapter_02_12_00/bitwise_exclusionary_or_with_acquisition_01/main.cpp

```cpp
1  #include <bitset>
2  #include <ciso646>
3  #include <iomanip>
4  #include <iostream>
5  #include <sstream>
6
7  const std::string LEFT                                        = "left";
8  const std::string RIGHT                                       = "right";
9  const std::string LEFT_PRIMARY_BITWISE_EXCLUSIONARY_OR_RIGHT  = LEFT + " ^= "
     + RIGHT;
10 const std::string LEFT_ALTERNATIVE_BITWISE_EXCLUSIONARY_OR_RIGHT = LEFT + "
     xor_eq " + RIGHT;
11
12 template <typename Operand_Type>
13 auto print(std::string const& operand_name, Operand_Type operand) {
14   std::stringstream result;
15
16   result << std::setw(LEFT_ALTERNATIVE_BITWISE_EXCLUSIONARY_OR_RIGHT.length())
17         << operand_name << " = " << std::dec << std::setw(sizeof(operand) * 3)
18         << +operand;
19   result << ", 0x" << std::setfill('0') << std::setw(sizeof(operand) * 2)
20         << std::uppercase << std::hex << +operand;
21   result << ", 0b" << std::bitset<sizeof(operand) * 8>(operand) << "\n";
22
23   return result;
24 }
25
26 typedef char Integer;
27
28 int main() {
29   Integer left;
30   Integer right;
```

```
31   long long input;
32
33   std::cout << "Please enter a \"" << LEFT << "\" operand:\n";
34   std::cin >> input;
35   left = static_cast<Integer>(input);
36   std::cout << "and a \"" << RIGHT << "\" operand:\n";
37   std::cin >> input;
38   right = static_cast<Integer>(input);
39
40   std::cout << std::endl;
41   std::cout << print(LEFT, left).rdbuf();
42   std::cout << print(RIGHT, right).rdbuf();
43
44   Integer result = left;
45   result ^= right;
46   std::cout
47      << print(LEFT_PRIMARY_BITWISE_EXCLUSIONARY_OR_RIGHT, result).rdbuf();
48
49   result = left;
50   result xor_eq right;
51   std::cout
52      << print(LEFT_ALTERNATIVE_BITWISE_EXCLUSIONARY_OR_RIGHT, result).rdbuf();
53
54   return EXIT_SUCCESS;
55 }
```

The above sample program demonstrates the use of the bitwise exclusion or assignment operator.

Listing 272. main.cpp#1

```
1 #include <bitset>
```

The include preprocessing loads **C++** definitions for bit manipulations in our case we use the std::bitset to output an integer to the binary format.

Listing 273. `main.cpp#2`

```
2 #include <ciso646>
```

The `include` preprocessing loads **C++** definitions for compatibility header, in C defines alternative operator representations which are keywords in **C++**.
This header was originally in the C standard library as `<iso646.h>`.
`<ciso646>` is removed in **C++20**.
Corresponding `<iso646.h>` is still available in **C++20**.

Listing 274. `main.cpp#3`

```
3 #include <iomanip>
```

The `include` preprocessing loads **C++** definitions for Input/Output (I/O) manipulators regarding formatiting of the stream I/O operations. We use manipulators like these:

- `std::dec` - next output is an decimal integer number;

- `std::setw` - set the width on a next output;

- `std::setfill` - set the fill character regarding difference between full width from the `std::setw` and real width of a printed value;

- `std::uppercase` - set the next output to be uppercase;
- `std::hex` - next output is an hexa decimal integer number.

Listing 275. `main.cpp#4`

```
4 #include <iostream>
```

The `include` preprocessing loads **C++** definitions for Input/Output (I/O) operations with streams.

In our program we use only:

- `std::cout` → output stream,
- `<<` → send right operand to the output stream (left operand) and
- `std::endl` → send `new line` to the output stream and flushes stream content.

Listing 276. `main.cpp#5`

```
5 #include <sstream>
```

The 'include' preprocessing command loads the definitions regarding string stream input and output operations.

Listing 277. `main.cpp#7..12`

```
 7 const std::string LEFT                                        = "left";
 8 const std::string RIGHT                                       = "right";
 9 const std::string LEFT_PRIMARY_BITWISE_EXCLUSIONARY_OR_RIGHT   = LEFT + " ^= "
   + RIGHT;
10 const std::string LEFT_ALTERNATIVE_BITWISE_EXCLUSIONARY_OR_RIGHT = LEFT + "
   xor_eq " + RIGHT;
11
12 template <typename Operand_Type>
```

The string constants declarations.

Listing 278. `main.cpp#14..26`

```
14     std::stringstream result;
15
16     result << std::setw(LEFT_ALTERNATIVE_BITWISE_EXCLUSIONARY_OR_RIGHT.length())
17            << operand_name << " = " << std::dec << std::setw(sizeof(operand) * 3)
18            << +operand;
19     result << ", 0x" << std::setfill('0') << std::setw(sizeof(operand) * 2)
20            << std::uppercase << std::hex << +operand;
21     result << ", 0b" << std::bitset<sizeof(operand) * 8>(operand) << "\n";
22
23     return result;
24 }
25
26 typedef char Integer;
```

Printing result of an operation.

Listing 279. `main.cpp#28`

```
28 int main() {
```

Integer warpper type definition - it can be used for covering different integer **C**++ types.

Listing 280. `main.cpp#30..57`

```
30   Integer right;
31   long long input;
32
33   std::cout << "Please enter a \"" << LEFT << "\" operand:\n";
34   std::cin >> input;
35   left = static_cast<Integer>(input);
36   std::cout << "and a \"" << RIGHT << "\" operand:\n";
37   std::cin >> input;
38   right = static_cast<Integer>(input);
39
40   std::cout << std::endl;
41   std::cout << print(LEFT, left).rdbuf();
42   std::cout << print(RIGHT, right).rdbuf();
43
44   Integer result = left;
45   result ^= right;
46   std::cout
47       << print(LEFT_PRIMARY_BITWISE_EXCLUSIONARY_OR_RIGHT, result).rdbuf();
48
49   result = left;
50   result xor_eq right;
51   std::cout
52       << print(LEFT_ALTERNATIVE_BITWISE_EXCLUSIONARY_OR_RIGHT, result).rdbuf();
53
54   return EXIT_SUCCESS;
55 }
```

This is the `main` function, which is the entry point into program execution. In it, the program simply reads two integers and performs the bitwise exclusive or assignment operation, using the basic and alternate bitwise exclusive operators, or outputs the result of both equivalent operations, the result should be the same.

4.13. logical_negation_01 / main.cpp

Listing 281.

~/c++/sources/chapter_02_13_00/logical_negation_01/main.cpp

```cpp
1  #include <bitset>
2  #include <ciso646>
3  #include <iomanip>
4  #include <iostream>
5  #include <sstream>
6
7  const std::string LEFT                                   = "left";
8  const std::string RIGHT                                  = "right";
9  const std::string LEFT_PRIMARY_LOGICAL_NEGATION_RIGHT    = "!" + RIGHT;
10 const std::string LEFT_ALTERNATIVE_LOGICAL_NEGATION_RIGHT = "not " + RIGHT;
11
12 template <typename Operand_Type>
13 auto print(std::string const& operand_name, Operand_Type operand) {
14    std::stringstream result;
15
16    result << std::setw(LEFT_ALTERNATIVE_LOGICAL_NEGATION_RIGHT.length())
17           << operand_name << " = " << std::dec << std::setw(sizeof(operand) * 3)
18           << +operand;
19    result << ", 0x" << std::setfill('0') << std::setw(sizeof(operand) * 2)
20           << std::uppercase << std::hex << +operand;
21    result << ", 0b" << std::bitset<sizeof(operand) * 8>(operand) << "\n";
22
23    return result;
24 }
25
26 typedef char Integer;
27
28 int main() {
29    Integer right;
30    long long input;
31
32    std::cout << "Please enter a \"" << RIGHT << "\" operand:\n";
33    std::cin >> input;
34    right = static_cast<Integer>(input);
35
36    std::cout << std::endl;
37    std::cout << print(RIGHT, right).rdbuf();
38    std::cout << print(LEFT_PRIMARY_LOGICAL_NEGATION_RIGHT,
39                       static_cast<Integer>(!right))
40                  .rdbuf();
```

```
41   std::cout << print(LEFT_ALTERNATIVE_LOGICAL_NEGATION_RIGHT,
42                 static_cast<Integer>(not right))
43              .rdbuf();
44
45   return EXIT_SUCCESS;
46 }
```

The above example program shows the use of the logical negation operator.

Listing 282. main.cpp#1

```
1 #include <bitset>
```

The include preprocessing loads **C++** definitions for bit manipulations in our case we use the std::bitset to output an integer to the binary format.

Listing 283. main.cpp#2

```
2 #include <ciso646>
```

The include preprocessing loads **C++** definitions for compatibility header, in C defines alternative operator representations which are keywords in **C++**.
This header was originally in the C standard library as <iso646.h>.
<ciso646> is removed in **C++20**.
Corresponding <iso646.h> is still available in **C++20**.

Listing 284. `main.cpp#3`

```
3 #include <iomanip>
```

The `include` preprocessing loads **C++** definitions for Input/Output (I/O) manipulators regarding formatiting of the stream I/O operations. We use manipulators like these:

- `std::dec` - next output is an decimal integer number;
- `std::setw` - set the width on a next output;
- `std::setfill` - set the fill character regarding difference between full width from the `std::setw` and real width of a printed value;
- `std::uppercase` - set the next output to be uppercase;
- `std::hex` - next output is an hexa decimal integer number.

Listing 285. `main.cpp#4`

```
4 #include <iostream>
```

The `include` preprocessing loads **C++** definitions for Input/Output (I/O) operations with streams.

In our program we use only:

- std::cout → output stream,

- << → send right operand to the output stream (left operand) and

- std::endl → send new line to the output stream and flushes stream content.

Listing 286. main.cpp#5

```
5 #include <sstream>
```

The 'include' preprocessing command loads the definitions regarding string stream input and output operations.

Listing 287. main.cpp#7..10

```
 7 const std::string LEFT                                  = "left";
 8 const std::string RIGHT                                 = "right";
 9 const std::string LEFT_PRIMARY_LOGICAL_NEGATION_RIGHT    = "!" + RIGHT;
10 const std::string LEFT_ALTERNATIVE_LOGICAL_NEGATION_RIGHT = "not " + RIGHT;
```

The string constants declarations.

Listing 288. main.cpp#12..24

```
12 template <typename Operand_Type>
13 auto print(std::string const& operand_name, Operand_Type operand) {
14   std::stringstream result;
15
16   result << std::setw(LEFT_ALTERNATIVE_LOGICAL_NEGATION_RIGHT.length())
17         << operand_name << " = " << std::dec << std::setw(sizeof(operand) * 3)
18         << +operand;
19   result << ", 0x" << std::setfill('0') << std::setw(sizeof(operand) * 2)
```

```
20            << std::uppercase << std::hex << +operand;
21   result << ", 0b" << std::bitset<sizeof(operand) * 8>(operand) << "\n";
22
23   return result;
24 }
```

Printing result of an operation.

Listing 289. main.cpp#26

```
26 typedef char Integer;
```

Integer warpper type definition - it can be used for covering different integer **C**++ types.

Listing 290. main.cpp#28..46

```
28 int main() {
29   Integer right;
30   long long input;
31
32   std::cout << "Please enter a \"" << RIGHT << "\" operand:\n";
33   std::cin >> input;
34   right = static_cast<Integer>(input);
35
36   std::cout << std::endl;
37   std::cout << print(RIGHT, right).rdbuf();
38   std::cout << print(LEFT_PRIMARY_LOGICAL_NEGATION_RIGHT,
39                      static_cast<Integer>(!right))
40                .rdbuf();
41   std::cout << print(LEFT_ALTERNATIVE_LOGICAL_NEGATION_RIGHT,
42                      static_cast<Integer>(not right))
43                .rdbuf();
44
45   return EXIT_SUCCESS;
46 }
```

This is the `main` function, which is the entry point into program execution. In it, the program simply reads an integer and performs the logical negation operation using the basic and alternate logical negation operators and outputs the result.

4.14.
logical_negation_with_acq uisition_01 / main.cpp

Listing 291.

~/c++/sources/chapter_02_14_00/logical_negation_with_acquisition_01/main
.cpp

```
1 #include <bitset>
2 #include <ciso646>
3 #include <iomanip>
4 #include <iostream>
5 #include <sstream>
6
7 const std::string LEFT                                    = "left";
8 const std::string RIGHT                                   = "right";
9 const std::string LEFT_PRIMARY_LOGICAL_NEGATION_RIGHT     = LEFT + "!=" + RIGHT;
10 const std::string LEFT_ALTERNATIVE_LOGICAL_NEGATION_RIGHT = LEFT + " not_eq " +
   RIGHT;
11
12 template <typename Operand_Type>
13 auto print(std::string const& operand_name, Operand_Type operand) {
14   std::stringstream result;
15
16   result << std::setw(LEFT_ALTERNATIVE_LOGICAL_NEGATION_RIGHT.length())
17         << operand_name << " = " << std::dec << std::setw(sizeof(operand) * 3)
18         << +operand;
19   result << ", 0x" << std::setfill('0') << std::setw(sizeof(operand) * 2)
20         << std::uppercase << std::hex << +operand;
21   result << ", 0b" << std::bitset<sizeof(operand) * 8>(operand) << "\n";
22
23   return result;
24 }
25
26 typedef char Integer;
27
28 int main() {
29   Integer left;
30   Integer right;
31   long long input;
32
33   std::cout << "Please enter a \"" << LEFT << "\" operand:\n";
34   std::cin >> input;
```

```
35    left = static_cast<Integer>(input);
36    std::cout << "and a \"" << RIGHT << "\" operand:\n";
37    std::cin >> input;
38    right = static_cast<Integer>(input);
39
40    std::cout << std::endl;
41    std::cout << print(LEFT, left).rdbuf();
42    std::cout << print(RIGHT, right).rdbuf();
43    std::cout << print(LEFT_PRIMARY_LOGICAL_NEGATION_RIGHT,
44                       static_cast<Integer>(left != right))
45                  .rdbuf();
46    std::cout << print(LEFT_ALTERNATIVE_LOGICAL_NEGATION_RIGHT,
47                       static_cast<Integer>(left not_eq right))
48                  .rdbuf();
49
50    return EXIT_SUCCESS;
51 }
```

The above example program shows the use of the logical negation operator with assignment.

Listing 292. main.cpp#1

```
1 #include <bitset>
```

The include preprocessing loads **C++** definitions for bit manipulations in our case we use the std::bitset to output an integer to the binary format.

Listing 293. main.cpp#2

```
2 #include <ciso646>
```

The include preprocessing loads **C++** definitions for compatibility header, in C defines alternative operator representations which are keywords in **C++**.

This header was originally in the C standard library as <iso646.h>.

<ciso646> is removed in **C++20**.

Corresponding <iso646.h> is still available in **C++20**.

Listing 294. main.cpp#3

```
3 #include <iomanip>
```

The include preprocessing loads **C++** definitions for Input/Output (I/O) manipulators regarding formatiting of the stream I/O operations. We use manipulators like these:

- std::dec - next output is an decimal integer number;

- std::setw - set the width on a next output;

- std::setfill - set the fill character regarding difference between full width from the std::setw and real width of a printed value;

- std::uppercase - set the next output to be uppercase;

- std::hex - next output is an hexa decimal integer number.

Listing 295. main.cpp#4

```
4 #include <iostream>
```

The `include` preprocessing loads **C++** definitions for Input/Output (I/O) operations with streams.

In our program we use only:

- `std::cout` → output stream,
- `<<` → send right operand to the output stream (left operand) and
- `std::endl` → send `new line` to the output stream and flushes stream content.

Listing 296. main.cpp#5

```
5 #include <sstream>
```

The 'include' preprocessing command loads the definitions regarding string stream input and output operations.

Listing 297. main.cpp#7..11

```
 7 const std::string LEFT                                  = "left";
 8 const std::string RIGHT                                 = "right";
 9 const std::string LEFT_PRIMARY_LOGICAL_NEGATION_RIGHT   = LEFT + "!=" + RIGHT;
10 const std::string LEFT_ALTERNATIVE_LOGICAL_NEGATION_RIGHT = LEFT + " not_eq " +
   RIGHT;
```

The string constants declarations.

Listing 298. main.cpp#13..25

```
13 auto print(std::string const& operand_name, Operand_Type operand) {
14    std::stringstream result;
15
16    result << std::setw(LEFT_ALTERNATIVE_LOGICAL_NEGATION_RIGHT.length())
17           << operand_name << " = " << std::dec << std::setw(sizeof(operand) * 3)
18           << +operand;
19    result << ", 0x" << std::setfill('0') << std::setw(sizeof(operand) * 2)
20           << std::uppercase << std::hex << +operand;
21    result << ", 0b" << std::bitset<sizeof(operand) * 8>(operand) << "\n";
22
23    return result;
24 }
```

Printing result of an operation.

Listing 299. main.cpp#27

Integer warpper type definition - it can be used for covering different integer C++ types.

Listing 300. main.cpp#29..52

```
29    Integer left;
30    Integer right;
31    long long input;
32
33    std::cout << "Please enter a \"" << LEFT << "\" operand:\n";
34    std::cin >> input;
35    left = static_cast<Integer>(input);
36    std::cout << "and a \"" << RIGHT << "\" operand:\n";
37    std::cin >> input;
38    right = static_cast<Integer>(input);
39
40    std::cout << std::endl;
41    std::cout << print(LEFT, left).rdbuf();
```

```
42    std::cout << print(RIGHT, right).rdbuf();
43    std::cout << print(LEFT_PRIMARY_LOGICAL_NEGATION_RIGHT,
44                    static_cast<Integer>(left != right))
45                .rdbuf();
46    std::cout << print(LEFT_ALTERNATIVE_LOGICAL_NEGATION_RIGHT,
47                    static_cast<Integer>(left not_eq right))
48                .rdbuf();
49
50    return EXIT_SUCCESS;
51 }
```

This is the `main` function, which is the entry point into program execution. In it, the program simply reads two integers and performs the logical negation with assignment operation, using the basic and alternative logical negation operators, and outputs the results, which must be the same.

...

4.15.
bitwise_compliment_01 / main.cpp

Listing 301.

~/c++/sources/chapter_02_15_00/bitwise_compliment_01/main.cpp

```cpp
#include <bitset>
#include <ciso646>
#include <iomanip>
#include <iostream>
#include <sstream>

const std::string RIGHT                                  = "right";
const std::string LEFT_PRIMARY_BITWISE_COMPLIMENT_RIGHT     = "~" + RIGHT;
const std::string LEFT_ALTERNATIVE_BITWISE_COMPLIMENT_RIGHT = "compl " + RIGHT;

template <typename Operand_Type>
auto print(std::string const& operand_name, Operand_Type operand) {
    std::stringstream result;

    result << std::setw(LEFT_ALTERNATIVE_BITWISE_COMPLIMENT_RIGHT.length()) //
           << operand_name                                                  //
           << " = "                                                         //
           << std::dec                                                      //
           << std::setw(sizeof(operand) * 3)                                //
           << +operand;                                                     //
    result << ", 0x"                                                        //
           << std::setfill('0')                                            //
           << std::setw(sizeof(operand) * 2)                                //
           << std::uppercase                                                //
           << std::hex                                                      //
           << +operand;                                                     //
    result << ", 0b"                                                        //
           << std::bitset<sizeof(operand) * 8>(operand)                     //
           << "\n";                                                         //

    return result;
}

class Primary_Compliment_Class {
  public:
    Primary_Compliment_Class() {
        std::cout << "Primary_Compliment_Class constructor\n";
```

```cpp
38    }
39    ~Primary_Compliment_Class() {
40      std::cout << "~Primary_Compliment_Class destructor\n";
41    }
42  };
43
44  class Alternative_Compliment_Class {
45  public:
46    Alternative_Compliment_Class() {
47      std::cout << "Alternative_Compliment_Class constructor\n";
48    }
49    compl Alternative_Compliment_Class() {
50      std::cout << "compl Alternative_Compliment_Class destructor\n";
51    }
52  };
53
54  struct Primary_Compliment_Structure {
55    Primary_Compliment_Structure() {
56      std::cout << "Primary_Compliment_Structure constructor\n";
57    }
58    ~Primary_Compliment_Structure() {
59      std::cout << "~Primary_Compliment_Structure destructor\n";
60    }
61  };
62
63  struct Alternative_Compliment_Structure {
64    Alternative_Compliment_Structure() {
65      std::cout << "Alternative_Compliment_Structure constructor\n";
66    }
67    compl Alternative_Compliment_Structure() {
68      std::cout << "compl Alternative_Compliment_Structure destructor\n";
69    }
70  };
71
72  typedef char Integer;
73
74  int main() {
75    Primary_Compliment_Class primary_compliment_class;
76    Alternative_Compliment_Class alternative_compliment_class;
77    Primary_Compliment_Structure primary_compliment_structure;
78    Alternative_Compliment_Structure alternative_compliment_structure;
79
80    Integer right;
81    long long input;
82
83    std::cout << "\nPlease enter a \"" << RIGHT << "\" operand:\n";
84    std::cin >> input;
85    right = static_cast<Integer>(input);
86
87    std::cout << std::endl;
88    std::cout << print(RIGHT, right).rdbuf();
89    std::cout << print(LEFT_PRIMARY_BITWISE_COMPLIMENT_RIGHT,
```

```
90                      static_cast<Integer>(~right))
91                  .rdbuf();
92    std::cout << print(LEFT_ALTERNATIVE_BITWISE_COMPLIMENT_RIGHT,
93                      static_cast<Integer>(compl right))
94                  .rdbuf();
95
96    std::cout << std::endl;
97
98    return EXIT_SUCCESS;
99 }
```

The above sample program demonstrates the use of the bitwise addition operator.

Listing 302. main.cpp#1

```
1 #include <bitset>
```

The include preprocessing loads **C++** definitions for bit manipulations in our case we use the std::bitset to output an integer to the binary format.

Listing 303. main.cpp#2

```
2 #include <ciso646>
```

The include preprocessing loads **C++** definitions for compatibility header, in C defines alternative operator representations which are keywords in **C++**.
This header was originally in the C standard library as <iso646.h>.

`<ciso646>` is removed in **C++20**.
Corresponding `<iso646.h>` is still available in **C++20**.

Listing 304. `main.cpp#3`

```
3 #include <iomanip>
```

The `include` preprocessing loads **C++** definitions for Input/Output (I/O) manipulators regarding formatiting of the stream I/O operations. We use manipulators like these:

- `std::dec` - next output is an decimal integer number;
- `std::setw` - set the width on a next output;
- `std::setfill` - set the fill character regarding difference between full width from the `std::setw` and real width of a printed value;
- `std::uppercase` - set the next output to be uppercase;
- `std::hex` - next output is an hexa decimal integer number.

Listing 305. `main.cpp#4`

```
4 #include <iostream>
```

The `include` preprocessing loads **C++** definitions for Input/Output (I/O) operations with streams.

In our program we use only:

- `std::cout` → output stream,
- `<<` → send right operand to the output stream (left operand) and
- `std::endl` → send `new` `line` to the output stream and flushes stream content.

Listing 306. main.cpp#5

```
5 #include <sstream>
```

The 'include' preprocessing command loads the definitions regarding string stream input and output operations.

Listing 307. main.cpp#7..9

```
7 const std::string RIGHT                                    = "right";
8 const std::string LEFT_PRIMARY_BITWISE_COMPLIMENT_RIGHT    = "~" + RIGHT;
9 const std::string LEFT_ALTERNATIVE_BITWISE_COMPLIMENT_RIGHT = "compl " + RIGHT;
```

The string constants declarations.

Listing 308. main.cpp#11..32

```
11 template <typename Operand_Type>
```

```
12 auto print(std::string const& operand_name, Operand_Type operand) {
13     std::stringstream result;
14
15     result << std::setw(LEFT_ALTERNATIVE_BITWISE_COMPLIMENT_RIGHT.length())  //
16            << operand_name                                                    //
17            << " = "                                                           //
18            << std::dec                                                        //
19            << std::setw(sizeof(operand) * 3)                                  //
20            << +operand;                                                       //
21     result << ", 0x"                                                          //
22            << std::setfill('0')                                              //
23            << std::setw(sizeof(operand) * 2)                                  //
24            << std::uppercase                                                  //
25            << std::hex                                                        //
26            << +operand;                                                       //
27     result << ", 0b"                                                          //
28            << std::bitset<sizeof(operand) * 8>(operand)                       //
29            << "\n";                                                           //
30
31     return result;
32 }
```

Printing result of an operation.

Listing 309. main.cpp#34..42

```
34 class Primary_Compliment_Class {
35   public:
36     Primary_Compliment_Class() {
37         std::cout << "Primary_Compliment_Class constructor\n";
38     }
39     ~Primary_Compliment_Class() {
40         std::cout << "~Primary_Compliment_Class destructor\n";
41     }
42 };
```

An example class whose destructor starts with a tilde (the basic bitwise padding operator). Destruct is one and matches the class name preceded by a tilde.

Listing 310. `main.cpp#44..52`

```
44 class Alternative_Compliment_Class {
45  public:
46   Alternative_Compliment_Class() {
47     std::cout << "Alternative_Compliment_Class constructor\n";
48   }
49   compl Alternative_Compliment_Class() {
50     std::cout << "compl Alternative_Compliment_Class destructor\n";
51   }
52 };
```

An example class whose destructor starts with `compl` (the alternative bitwise complement operator). Destruct is one and matches the class name preceded by a tilde or the alternative bitwise complement operator `compl`.

Listing 311. `main.cpp#54..61`

```
54 struct Primary_Compliment_Structure {
55   Primary_Compliment_Structure() {
56     std::cout << "Primary_Compliment_Structure constructor\n";
57   }
58   ~Primary_Compliment_Structure() {
59     std::cout << "~Primary_Compliment_Structure destructor\n";
60   }
61 };
```

An example structure whose destructor starts with a tilde (the basic bitwise padding operator). Destruct is one and corresponds to the name of the structure preceded by a tilde. The main difference between a class and a struct is that all members of a class are private by default and of a struct are public by default.

Listing 312. `main.cpp#63..70`

```
63 struct Alternative_Compliment_Structure {
64   Alternative_Compliment_Structure() {
65     std::cout << "Alternative_Compliment_Structure constructor\n";
66   }
67   compl Alternative_Compliment_Structure() {
68     std::cout << "compl Alternative_Compliment_Structure destructor\n";
69   }
70 };
```

An example structure whose destructor begins with the `compl` (the alternative bitwise complement operator). Destruct is one and matches the name of the structure preceded by a tilde or the alternative bitwise complement operator `compl`.

Listing 313. `main.cpp#72`

```
72 typedef char Integer;
```

Integer warpper type definition - it can be used for covering different integer **C**++ types.

Listing 314. `main.cpp#74..99`

```
74 int main() {
75   Primary_Compliment_Class primary_compliment_class;
76   Alternative_Compliment_Class alternative_compliment_class;
77   Primary_Compliment_Structure primary_compliment_structure;
78   Alternative_Compliment_Structure alternative_compliment_structure;
79
80   Integer right;
81   long long input;
82
```

```
83    std::cout << "\nPlease enter a \"" << RIGHT << "\" operand:\n";
84    std::cin >> input;
85    right = static_cast<Integer>(input);

86
87    std::cout << std::endl;
88    std::cout << print(RIGHT, right).rdbuf();
89    std::cout << print(LEFT_PRIMARY_BITWISE_COMPLIMENT_RIGHT,
90                       static_cast<Integer>(~right))
91                  .rdbuf();
92    std::cout << print(LEFT_ALTERNATIVE_BITWISE_COMPLIMENT_RIGHT,
93                       static_cast<Integer>(compl right))
94                  .rdbuf();

95
96    std::cout << std::endl;

97
98    return EXIT_SUCCESS;
99 }
```

This is the main function, which is the entry point into program execution. At the beginning of it, we create sample and alternative classes and structures, which at the end call their destructors. The program then simply reads two integers and performs the bitwise addition operation using the basic and alternate bitwise addition operators and outputs the results, which should be the same.

4.16.
comment_to_the_end_of_li ne_01 / main.cpp

Listing 315.

~/c++/sources/chapter_03_01_00/comment_to_the_end_of_line_01/main.cpp

```cpp
 1 #include <cstdlib>   // <-- EXIT_SUCCESS
 2 #include <iostream>  // <-- std::cout, <<, std::endl
 3
 4 namespace comments {
 5
 6 void print_message(std::string message) {
 7   // Output message to the console:
 8   std::cout << message << std::endl;
 9 }
10
11 } // namespace comments
12 using namespace comments;
13
14 // Following function 'main' is an entry point to the C++ program:
15 int main() {
16   print_message("Hello from comment to the end of current line '//'");
17
18   // Exiting with the success status --> '0':
19   return EXIT_SUCCESS;
20 }
```

The above program demonstrates different options for using a comment at the end of the // line.

Listing 316. main.cpp#1

```cpp
 1 #include <cstdlib>   // <-- EXIT_SUCCESS
```

The `include` preprocessing loads **C++** definitions for `EXIT_SUCCESS` and `EXIT_FAILURE` also all **C** definitions from `<stdlib.h>` include file.

Listing 317. `main.cpp#2`

```
2 #include <iostream>  // <-- std::cout, <<, std::endl
```

The `include` preprocessing loads **C++** definitions for Input/Output (I/O) operations with streams.

In our program we use only:

- `std::cout` → output stream,
- `<<` → send right operand to the output stream (left operand) and
- `std::endl` → send `new line` to the output stream and flushes stream content.

Listing 318. `main.cpp#4`

```
4 namespace comments {
```

Start of `comments` namespace. All components defined in a namespace can be accessed outside of it by using the namespace and a double colon before the name of the defined component. For example `comments::print_message(···);` When we want to access the components without explicitly specifying the namespace name, we simply set it like `using namespace comments;`, after this definition we can access the components from the namespace through their names. For example `print_message(···);`

Listing 319. `main.cpp#6..9`

```
6 void print_message(std::string message) {
7   // Output message to the console:
8   std::cout << message << std::endl;
9 }
```

Function to print a text message defined in the `comments` namespace.

Listing 320. `main.cpp#11..12`

```
11 }  // namespace comments
12 using namespace comments;
```

End `comments` namespace and specify its default usage, that is, components defined in it are accessible without explicitly specifying the namespace name and a double colon in front of the component names.

Listing 321. `main.cpp#14..20`

```
14 // Following function `main` is an entry point to the C++ program:
15 int main() {
16   print_message("Hello from comment to the end of current line '//'");
```

```
 17
 18    // Exiting with the success status --> `0`;
 19    return EXIT_SUCCESS;
 20 }
```

Defining the entry point in the program - the function `main`. This function simply outputs a message and successfully completes its execution. The main part demonstrates various end-of-line comments starting with `//`. Everything after the beginning of the commas to the end of the line is ignored by the **C++** compiler and is intended to document the program code as well as to facilitate code changes.

4.17. multiline_comment_01 / main.cpp

Listing 322.

~/c++/sources/chapter_03_02_00/multiline_comment_01/main.cpp

```cpp
 1 #include <cstdlib> /* <-- EXIT_SUCCESS */
 2 #include <iostream> /* <-- std::cout, <<, std::endln */
 3
 4 namespace comments {
 5
 6 void print_message(std::string message) {
 7   /*
 8    Output message
 9    to the console:
10   */
11   std::cout << message << std::endl;
12 }
13
14 } // namespace comments
15 using namespace comments;
16
17 /*
18  Following function `main`
19  is an entry point to the C++ program:
20 */
21 int main() {
22   print_message("Hello from the multiline comment '/* ... */'");
23
24   /*
25    Exiting with the success status --> '0':
26   */
27   return EXIT_SUCCESS;
28 }
```

The above program demonstrates different options for using multiline comments starting with /* and ending with */.

Listing 323. main.cpp#1

```
1 #include <cstdlib>  /* <-- EXIT_SUCCESS */
```

The include preprocessing loads **C++** definitions for EXIT_SUCCESS and EXIT_FAILURE also all **C** definitions from <stdlib.h> include file.

Listing 324. main.cpp#2

```
2 #include <iostream> /* <-- std::cout, <<, std::endln */
```

The include preprocessing loads **C++** definitions for Input/Output (I/O) operations with streams.

In our program we use only:

- std::cout → output stream,
- << → send right operand to the output stream (left operand) and
- std::endl → send new line to the output stream and flushes stream content.

Listing 325. main.cpp#4

```
4 namespace comments {
```

Start of comments namespace. All components defined in a namespace can be accessed outside of it by using the namespace and a double colon before the name of the defined component. For example `comments::print_message(···);` When we want to access the components without explicitly specifying the namespace name, we simply set it like `using namespace comments;`, after this definition we can access the components from the namespace through their names. For example `print_message(···);`

Listing 326. `main.cpp#6..12`

```
 6 void print_message(std::string message) {
 7   /*
 8     Output message
 9     to the console:
10   */
11     std::cout << message << std::endl;
12 }
```

Function to print a text message defined in the `comments` namespace.

Listing 327. `main.cpp#14..15`

```
14 }  // namespace comments
15 using namespace comments;
```

End `comments` namespace and specify its default usage, that is, components defined in it are accessible without explicitly specifying the namespace name and a double colon in front of the component names.

Listing 328. `main.cpp#17..28`

```
17  /*
18  Following function 'main'
19  is an entry point to the C++ program:
20  */
21  int main() {
22    print_message("Hello from the multiline comment '/* ... */'");
23
24    /*
25    Exiting with the success status --> '0':
26    */
27    return EXIT_SUCCESS;
28  }
```

Defining the entry point in the program - the function `main`. This function simply outputs a message and successfully completes its execution. The main part is to demonstrate various multiline comments starting with /* and ending with */. Anything between /* and */ is ignored by the **C++** compiler and is intended to document the program code as well as to make it easier for programmers.

4.18.
multiline_preprocessing_c omment_01 / main.cpp

Listing 329.
~/c++/sources/chapter_03_03_00/multiline_preprocessing_comment_01/main.c
pp

```cpp
1 #include <cstdlib>   // <-- EXIT_SUCCESS
2 #include <iostream>  // <-- std::cout, <<, std::endln
3
4 #if 0
5
6 namespace comments {
7
8 void print_message(std::string message) {
9   // Output message to the console:
10   std::cout << message << std::endl;
11 }
12
13 }  // namespace comments
14 using namespace comments;
15
16 #endif  // 0
17
18 #ifdef COMMENT
19
20 namespace comments {
21
22 void print_message(const char* message) {
23   // Output message to the console:
24   std::cout << message << std::endl;
25 }
26
27 }  // namespace comments
28 using namespace comments;
29
30 #endif  // COMMENT
31
32 void print_message(std::string const& message) {
33   // Output message to the console:
34   std::cout << message << std::endl;
35 }
```

```
36
37  /*
38   Following function `main`
39   is an entry point to the C++ program:
40  */
41  int main() {
42    print_message("Hello from the multiline preprocessing comment");
43
44    // Exiting with the success status --> `0`:
45    return EXIT_SUCCESS;
46  }
```

The above program demonstrates different options for using multiline comments using the preprocessor definitions #if or #ifdef (you can also use #ifndef respectively) and ending with #endif.

Listing 330. main.cpp#1

```
1 #include <cstdlib>   // <-- EXIT_SUCCESS
```

The include preprocessing loads C++ definitions for EXIT_SUCCESS and EXIT_FAILURE also all C definitions from <stdlib.h> include file.

Listing 331. main.cpp#2

```
2 #include <iostream>  // <-- std::cout, <<, std::endl
```

The include preprocessing loads C++ definitions for Input/Output (I/O) operations with streams.

In our program we use only:

- `std::cout` → output stream,

- `<<` → send right operand to the output stream (left operand) and

- `std::endl` → send `new line` to the output stream and flushes stream content.

Listing 332. `main.cpp#4`

```
4 #if 0
```

We can ignore any part of **C++** program code using `#if 0` because the conditional preprocessor statement ignores everything after it until `#endif` or `#else` when the condition it checks is equal to zero `0`. This way we can easily comment out large chunks of code that include other comments or even nested `#if` ... `#endif` constructs.

Listing 333. `main.cpp#6`

```
6 namespace comments {
```

Start of `comments` namespace. All components defined in a namespace can be accessed outside of it by using the namespace and a double colon before the name of the defined component. For example `comments::print_message(···);` When we want to access the components without explicitly specifying the namespace name, we simply set it like `using namespace comments;`, after this definition we can access the components from the namespace through their names. For example `print_message(···);`

Listing 334. `main.cpp#8..11`

```
8  void print_message(std::string message) {
9    // Output message to the console:
10   std::cout << message << std::endl;
11 }
```

Function to print a text message defined in the `comments` namespace.

Listing 335. `main.cpp#13..14`

```
13 } // namespace comments
14 using namespace comments;
```

End `comments` namespace and specify its default usage, that is, components defined in it are accessible without explicitly specifying the namespace name and a double colon in front of the component names.

Listing 336. `main.cpp#16`

```
16 #endif  // 0
```

End of multiline comment (conditional preprocessor statement) starting with `#if 0`.

Listing 337. `main.cpp#18`

```
18 #ifdef COMMENT
```

We can ignore any part of **C++** program code using `#ifdef COMMENT` when `COMMENT` is not a defined name, because the conditional preprocessor statement ignores everything after it until `#endif` or ` #else` when the definition preprocessor name it checks for is not defined. This way we can easily comment out large chunks of code that include other comments or even nested `#if/#ifdef/#ifndef` ... `#endif` constructs.

Listing 338. `main.cpp#20`

```
20 namespace comments {
```

Start of `comments` namespace. All components defined in a namespace can be accessed outside of it by using the namespace and a double colon before the name of the defined component. For example `comments::print_message(⋯);` When we want to access the components without explicitly specifying the namespace name, we simply set it like `using namespace comments;`, after this definition we can access the components from the namespace through their names. For example `print_message(···);`

Listing 339. `main.cpp#22..25`

```
22  void print_message(const char* message) {
23    // Output message to the console:
24    std::cout << message << std::endl;
25  }
```

Function to print a text message defined in the `comments` namespace.

Listing 340. `main.cpp#27..28`

```
27  } // namespace comments
28  using namespace comments;
```

End `comments` namespace and specify its default usage, that is, components defined in it are accessible without explicitly specifying the namespace name and a double colon in front of the component names.

Listing 341. main.cpp#30

```
30 #endif  // COMMENT
```

End of multiline comment (conditional preprocessor statement) starting with #ifdef COMMENT.

Listing 342. main.cpp#32..35

```
32 void print_message(std::string const& message) {
33   // Output message to the console:
34   std::cout << message << std::endl;
35 }
```

The above function simply prints out a text message.

Listing 343. main.cpp#37..46

```
37 /*
38  Following function `main`
39  is an entry point to the C++ program:
40 */
41 int main() {
42   print_message("Hello from the multiline preprocessing comment");
43
44   // Exiting with the success status --> `0`:
45   return EXIT_SUCCESS;
46 }
```

The main function is the entry point into the **C++** program and prints a text message to the screen using the print_message function, then completes its execution successfully (that is, returns 0 - an `EXIT_SUCCESS` success status).

Appendix A: Installing a newer release version of the GNU Compiler Collection (GCC)

 Keep the following feature in mind before you decide to install this version!

Compiling and installing **GCC** from the source can take several hours.

1. First, we need to update the version of **Linux**:

Listing 344. Linux Terminal

```
sudo apt -y update
```

2. Next, we install the tools, by default for the version of the **Linux Ubuntu** operating system used, to compile **C/C++** programs.

Listing 345. Linux Terminal

```
sudo apt -y install build-essential
```

3. We also will install the following two applications - `flex` and `bison`, which are used when compiling **GCC**.

Listing 346. Linux Terminal

```
sudo apt -y install flex
sudo apt -y install bison
```

4. We enter the root folder of the current **Linux** user.

Listing 347. Linux Terminal

```
cd ~
```

5. We download the archive containing the relevant **GCC** release version and unzip it.

Listing 348. Linux Terminal

```
wget -nc \
   https://bigsearcher.com/mirrors/gcc/releases/gcc-12.2.0/gcc-12.2.0.tar.gz

tar xvzf gcc-12.2.0.tar.gz
```

 You can look at https://bigsearcher.com/mirrors/gcc/releases for a newer version.

6. We go into the just unzipped folder containing the **GCC** release.

Listing 349. Linux Terminal

```
cd gcc-12.2.0
```

7. We download the necessary dependencies to compile **GCC**.

Listing 350. Linux Terminal

```
./contrib/download_prerequisites
```

8. We export two environment variables `LIBRARY_PATH` and `LD_LIBRARY_PATH` which are required when compiling **GCC**.

Listing 351. Linux Terminal

```
export LIBRARY_PATH=/usr/lib64
export LD_LIBRARY_PATH=/usr/lib64
```

9. We create the `build` folder that we will use to build the applications from **GCC** and then enter it.

Listing 352. Linux Terminal

```
mkdir build
cd build/
```

10. We configure the system so that its creation is possible.

Listing 353. Linux Terminal

```
../configure --prefix=/usr/local/gxx-12 --disable-multilib
```

11. Starting the **GCC** build process.

Listing 354. Linux Terminal

```
time make -j $(nproc)
```

 It may take several hours depending on the power of the computer on which we run it.

12. We start the process of installing the already compiled **GCC** applications.

Listing 355. Linux Terminal

```
sudo make install
```

13. We check the current version of g++

Listing 356. Linux Terminal

```
g++ --version
```

Example 41. The command displays the current version of g++ and the result is something like this:

```
g++ (Ubuntu 11.3.0-1ubuntu1~22.04) 11.3.0
Copyright (C) 2021 Free Software Foundation, Inc.
This is free software; see the source for copying conditions.   There is
NO
warranty; not even for MERCHANTABILITY or FITNESS FOR A PARTICULAR
PURPOSE.
```

14. We insert the path to the applications from the newly built **GCC** at the beginning of the

PATH environment variable, append it to the end of the ~/.bashrc file, and finally enable the contents of this file again, enabling the new value of the PATH variable.

Listing 357. Linux Terminal

```
cd ~
echo -e "\nPATH=/usr/local/gxx-12/bin:\$PATH" >> .bashrc
source .bashrc
```

15. Again we check the current version of C++ and it should match the newly built one.

Listing 358. Linux Terminal

```
g++ --version
```

Example 42. The command displays the latest version of **GCC**, *and the result of it is something like this:*

```
g++ (GCC) 12.2.0
Copyright (C) 2022 Free Software Foundation, Inc.
This is free software; see the source for copying conditions.  There is
NO
warranty; not even for MERCHANTABILITY or FITNESS FOR A PARTICULAR
PURPOSE.
```

This completes the installation of a newer release version of **GCC**.

Appendix B: Installing the latest version of the GNU Compiler Collection (GCC)

Keep the following features in mind before you decide to install this version!

1. Compiling and installing **GCC** from the source can take several hours.
2. The latest version of **GCC** is experimental and may sometimes not compile or work completely as expected.

1. First, we need to update the version of **Linux**:

Listing 359. Linux Terminal

```
sudo apt -y update
```

2. Next, we install the tools, by default for the

version of the **Linux Ubuntu** operating system used, to compile **C/C++** programs.

Listing 360. Linux Terminal

```
sudo apt -y install build-essential
```

3. We also will install the version control system **git**, with which we will download the repository containing the latest version of **GCC**.

Listing 361. Linux Terminal

```
sudo apt -y install git
```

4. We also will install the following two applications - `flex` and `bison`, which are used when compiling **GCC**.

Listing 362. Linux Terminal

```
sudo apt -y install flex
sudo apt -y install bison
```

5. We enter the root folder of the current **Linux** user.

Listing 363. Linux Terminal

```
cd ~
```

6. We download the repository containing the latest version of **GCC**.

Listing 364. Linux Terminal

```
git clone git://gcc.gnu.org/git/gcc.git
```

7. We go into the **GCC** source code repository we just downloaded.

Listing 365. Linux Terminal

```
cd gcc/
```

8. We download the necessary dependencies to compile **GCC**.

Listing 366. Linux Terminal

```
./contrib/download_prerequisites
```

9. We export two environment variables LIBRARY_PATH and LD_LIBRARY_PATH which are required when compiling **GCC**.

Listing 367. Linux Terminal

```
export LIBRARY_PATH=/usr/lib64
export LD_LIBRARY_PATH=/usr/lib64
```

10. We create the build folder that we will use to build the applications from **GCC** and then enter it.

Listing 368. Linux Terminal

```
mkdir build
cd build/
```

11. We configure the system so that its creation is possible.

Listing 369. Linux Terminal

```
../configure --prefix=/usr/local/gxx-13 --disable-multilib
```

12. Starting the **GCC** build process.

Listing 370. Linux Terminal

```
time make -j $(nproc)
```

It may take several hours depending on the power of the computer on which we run it. The build process may fail as this is an experimental release, so you must switch to a transient tag from the git repository.

13. We start the process of installing the already compiled **GCC** applications.

Listing 371. Linux Terminal

```
sudo make install
```

14. We check the current version of g++.

Listing 372. Linux Terminal

```
g++ --version
```

Example 43. The command displays the current version of g++ *and the result is something like this:*

```
g++ (Ubuntu 11.3.0-1ubuntu1~22.04) 11.3.0
Copyright (C) 2021 Free Software Foundation, Inc.
This is free software; see the source for copying conditions.  There is
NO
warranty; not even for MERCHANTABILITY or FITNESS FOR A PARTICULAR
PURPOSE.
```

15. We insert the path to the applications from the newly built **GCC** at the beginning of the PATH environment variable, append it to the end of the ~/.bashrc file, and finally enable the contents of this file again, enabling the new value of the PATH variable.

Listing 373. Linux Terminal

```
cd ~
echo -e "\nPATH=/usr/local/gxx-13/bin:\$PATH" >> .bashrc
source .bashrc
```

16. Again we will check the current version of the C++ compiler and it should match the newly built one.

Listing 374. Linux Terminal

```
g++ --version
```

Example 44. The command displays the latest version of **GCC**, *and the result of it is something like this:*

```
g++ (GCC) 14.0.1 20240130 (experimental)
```

This completes the installation of the latest experimental version of **GCC**.

About the Author

Eng. Zlatin Georgiev

https://www.linkedin.com/in/zlatin-georgiev/

Dear reader,
You can write about this book to Zlatin Georgiev

by e-mail:
zlatin.v.g@gmail.com

with the subject:
Fast and Easy C++ Lessons: In This Edition: Alternative Tokens and Comments On Microsoft Visual Studio Code in Linux Ubuntu

Of course, the author will not be able to respond to all e-mails, but he will consider your recommendations regarding the content of this book if possible.

Other books from the series til now

- Fast and Easy C++ Lessons: In This Edition Alternative Tokens and Comments On Microsoft Visual Studio Code in Linux Ubuntu
- Fast and Easy C++ Lessons: In This Edition Alternative Tokens and Comments On Microsoft Visual Studio Code in Windows
- Fast and Easy C++ Lessons: In This Edition Bitwise Operators On Microsoft Visual Studio Code in Linux Ubuntu
- Fast and Easy C++ Lessons: In This Edition Bitwise Operators On Microsoft Visual Studio Code in Windows
- Fast and Easy C++ Lessons: In This Edition Character Sets On Microsoft Visual Studio Code in Linux Ubuntu
- Fast and Easy C++ Lessons: In This Edition Character Sets On Microsoft Visual Studio Code in Windows
- Fast and Easy C++ Lessons: In This Edition Preprocessing On Microsoft Visual Studio Code in Linux Ubuntu
- Fast and Easy C++ Lessons: In This Edition

All books have the following formats:

1. Color interior:
    - Kindle
    - Paperback
    - Hardcover
2. Black and white interior:
    - Paperback
    - Hardcover